The New Atlantis and The City of the Sun

TWO CLASSIC UTOPIAS

Francis Bacon
and
Tomasso Campanella

Dover Publications, Inc.
Mineola, New York

CONTENTS

Introduction   iii

The New Atlantis   1

The City of the Sun   41

Bibliographical Note

This Dover edition, first published in 2003, is an unabridged republication of *The New Atlantis* by Francis Bacon and *The City of the Sun* by Tomasso Campanella, as originally published in *Famous Utopias: Being the Complete Text of Rousseau's* Social Contract, *More's* Utopia, *Bacon's* New Atlantis, [and] *Campanella's* City of the Sun by Tudor Publishing Co., New York, in 1901. The original 1901 introduction, written by Charles M. Andrews, has been abridged and adapted for the Dover edition.

Library of Congress Cataloging-in-Publication Data

Bacon, Francis, 1561–1626.
    The New Atlantis / Francis Bacon. And The City of the Sun / Tomasso Campanella.
        p. cm.
    "Two classic utopias."
    "Reprinted from standard texts"—T.p. verso.
    ISBN 0-486-43082-0 (pbk.)
      1. Utopias—Early works to 1800. I. Campanella, Tomasso, 1568–1639. Civitas Solis. English. II. Title: City of the Sun. III. Title.

HX811.B33 2003
335'.02—dc21   2003046193

Manufactured in the United States of America
Dover Publications, Inc., 31 East 2nd Street, Mineola, N.Y. 11501

INTRODUCTION

THE TERM Utopia, as generally used, refers to those ideal states which are impossible of realization, both because they are peopled by ideal human beings uninfluenced by personal jealousies or individual passions, and because they are based, with but little regard for the complexities and varieties of real society, upon what the writer thinks ought to be, rather than upon the collective experience of mankind. More broadly speaking, however, the term need not be confined to these "fantastic pictures of impossible societies," or "romantic accounts of fictitious states," as they have been called, but may be applied to any social, intellectual, or political scheme which is impracticable at the time when it is conceived and presented. Thus enlarged, the field may be made to include schemes as diverse as More's *Utopia,* Campanella's *City of the Sun,* Cabet's *Icarie,* and Morris's *News from Nowhere;* Rousseau's society of the *Social Contract;* and modern socialistic and communistic organizations, such as the *Co-operative Commonwealth* of Lawrence Grönlund, popularized by Bellamy in *Looking Backward,* and Flürcheim's *Money Island.*

Utopias have generally made their appearance during periods of great social and political unrest, and it is, therefore, no accident that after Plato's *Republic,* written during dark days in the history of Athens, all Utopias should have fallen in the period from the beginning of the sixteenth century to the present time. The Middle Ages, with their fixed institutions, their blind faith, and their acceptance of authority were not a suitable seed-ground for the growth of Utopian schemes. Any ideals that were conceived were of a religious character, based upon conceptions of the past and hopes of the future: those of the past combined the pagan notion of a golden age with the Christian's concept of an age of innocence, giving rise to the doctrine that man had fallen from a perfect life whose simple rules were based on natural law; those of the future looked forward to the re-establishment of Christ's kingdom on earth. Such doctrines were characteristic of a period in which there existed no true idea of human progress.

But in the period following the Middle Ages, when mediæval institutions were breaking down and men were awakening to the fact that governments had become corrupt and tyrannical, and social relations unjust and immoral, it was natural that they should find comfort and satisfaction in casting into romantic or ideal form their conception of what society ought to be. Excellent examples of such Utopias are to be found among the works of sixteenth century writers, who prompted by the new spirit of inquiry constructed ideal conditions that should eliminate the evils of their age. The earliest, More's *Utopia* (1516), presents the lofty ideals of the Oxford reformers, and stands as the greatest literary effort of the time; Vives, a versatile Catholic humanist, in 1531 erected in his *De Corruptis Artibus* and *De Tradendis Discipliniis* an ideal academy, a pedagogical Utopia, founded on the highest educational, scientific, and moral considerations;* Doni in *I Mundi celesti, terrestri, et infernali* (1552–53) satirized in Utopian form the political and social vices of Italy; and a little later, in 1605, under the pseudonym, Mercurius Britannicus, Joseph Hall, made Bishop of Norwich in 1641, published a moral satire, *Mundus Alter et Idem,* in tone rather Rabelaisian than ideal.

As the seventeenth century advanced, the spirit of free inquiry grew bolder, overthrowing the philosophy of Aristotle, and leading men to study the operations of nature in order to discover the fundamental principles that underlay the constitution of the universe. Three writers, in harmony with the spirit of the age, conceived philosophical and intellectual Utopias, in which by means of the new methods of scientific experimentation the social and intellectual order was to be remodeled. Campanella, a Dominican monk of Calabria, began in 1602 his *Civitas Solis,* which he published

---

Handbuch der Pädagogik, Vol. VII., p. 425.

in 1623; Bacon in the *Novus Atlantis,* written before 1617 and published in 1627, exhibited a state of which the most striking feature was a college "instituted for the interpreting of nature and the production of great and marvelous works for the benefit of man;" and Comenius, after issuing his *Conatuum Pansophicorum Dilucidatio* in 1639, went to England to form a "Universal College" for physical research on the lines suggested by Bacon in the *New Atlantis.** But in the turmoil of the Civil War the *Pansophia* of Comenius was lost, and hopes of a Universal College soon vanished.

During the next hundred years political questions supplanted philosophical. Harrington's *Oceana* dedicated to Cromwell in 1656, was not a romance, but "the first sketch in English political science of a written constitution limiting sovereignty,"† "the only valuable model of a commonwealth," as Hume calls it. Hume himself, a century later (1752), in his *Essays, Moral and Political,* Part II., commenting on Plato, More, and Harrington, presented his "Idea of a Perfect Commonwealth," and believed that in his *Utopia* he had discovered a form of government to which he himself could not in theory formulate "any considerable objection."

In France also, writers were coming forward with schemes of a perfect government. Vairasse d'Allais, in *La République des Sévarambes,* a part of his *Histoire des Sévarambes,* 1672, pictured a monarchy, with the state owning land and wealth and the people dwelling in huge osmasies like Fourier's *phalanstères.* Fénélon in Book X. of the *Télémaque,* which contains his account of the kingdom of Salente, described a perfect state under the authority of a perfect king.

But Utopias advocating monarchy are rare. With the realization of the evils of the state system of the eighteenth century, thought took a new direction. Morelly in *Naufrage des îles flottantes ou la Basiliade de Pilpai,* 1753, declared that the existing conditions were corrupt, attacked the law of property, and tried to demonstrate the necessity of placing society under the law of nature and truth,—ideas more fully developed in his *Code de la Nature,* 1755. This appeal to the law of nature showed the prevailing political concept of the

---

*Keatinge: *The Great Didactic of Comenius,* p. 45.
†Dwight in "Political Science Quarterly," 1887, p. 17.

period. The eyes of the reformers were now turned to the natural principles of social order and government, and in 1762 Rousseau gave to the world, in the *Contrat Social* his scheme of the state founded on social compact. Mably went further than Rousseau, and in his various writings from 1765 to 1784 denounced private property, inheritance and right of bequest, commerce, credit, the arts and sciences, libraries, museums, and the like. Finding his ideal among the Greeks, he viewed the Spartan era as a golden age, and extolled poverty as the mother of frugality and the virtues. He preached not only equality and equal education for all, but a federal state and community of goods. If Rousseau inspired Robespierre and St. Just, it is equally true that Mably and Pechméja (*Télèphe,* 1784) inspired Marat, Babœuf, and Buonarrotti. Although during the French Revolution men acted rather than dreamed, yet in the teachings of Maréchal, Marat, and the Girondist Brissot de Warville, and in the speeches of St. Just and Robespierre, we find embodied Utopian ideals regarding man and his fundamental rights. The adoption of the constitution of 1793 was as truly an attempt to found a Utopia as was the forming of the "Society of Equals," through which Babœuf hoped to hasten a communistic millennium.

The French Revolution so shattered society that writers of Utopias, who before had had little real expectation of seeing their theories applied, now worked to remodel the social and industrial order. The followers of St. Simon established an experimental community in 1826; in 1840 a *phalanstère* of Fourier was set up at Brook Farm in America; at New Lanark, before the close of the eighteenth century, Robert Owen had tried his economic Utopia, and in 1825 was experimenting at New Harmony in Pennsylvania. In 1848 great national workshops were set up in Paris; and in Algiers Marshal Bugeaud endeavored to establish a military colony on a communistic basis. Cabet copied More's *Utopia* in his *Voyage en Icarie,* and gave it a better trial at Nauvoo in Illinois in 1849 than had Frank, Münster, and Münzer in Germany in the sixteenth century. But after Cabet's *Icarie,* except in a few cases such as Lytton's *Coming Race,* Bellamy's *Looking Backward,* and Secrétan's *Mon Utopie,* which were little more than literary pastimes, and such experimental communities as the Christian Commonwealth near Columbus, Georgia, and the Ruskin Colony in the same state, both of which have failed, the history of Utopias is the history of scientific socialism, and is not to be dealt with here.

Both Campanella's *City of the Sun* and Bacon's *New Atlantis,* notwithstanding their differences in setting and treatment, represent an awakened interest in a new philosophy. Unlike Sir Thomas More, neither Campanella nor Bacon concerned himself much with the economic or social questions of his time. Campanella was from boyhood a student of logic and physics. Bacon, led partly by personal inclination, and partly by the fact that in the greater prosperity of the age of Elizabeth, social conditions had become less exigent, turned his attention to politics and philosophy. The crisis reflected in the Utopias of these writers were, therefore, revolutions, not in society, but in philosophical thought and method. Influenced by Bernhard Telesius (1508–88), the great Italian opponent of the doctrines of Aristotle, Campanella, like Bacon saw the need of a fundamental reform of natural philosophy, and the substitution for analogies and abstract generalizations of the sounder method of exact observation. Unwilling to employ principles established arbitrarily, they based all conclusions on careful and scientific experimentation. Before Campanella was twenty-five years old he had published a series of works supporting the contention that men can understand the world only through the senses. Bacon, born in 1561, seven years earlier than Campanella, although from boyhood eager to accomplish by means of a new philosophy something of practical benefit for humanity, was slower in publishing his views. Whereas the *City of the Sun,* written after the *De Sensu Rerum, Philosophia Sensibus Demonstrata,* and *De Investigatione Rerum,* presents a social and philosophical scheme worked out in minute detail, the *New Atlantis,* written before the publication of the *Novum Organum* and the *Instauratio Magna,* is but a sketch of the results Bacon would like to have attained, rather than a demonstration of the methods necessary for their attainment. Campanella's work is, so far as it goes, complete; Bacon's is only a fragment which probably he never intended to perfect.

Campanella, born in southern Calabria in 1568, became

at a very early age a Dominican monk and was interested rather in physics than in theology. By attacking the prevailing Aristotelian philosophy, he soon roused enemies against him, and was imprisoned on the charge of conspiring to overthrow the Kingdom of Naples and found a republic. He was seven times tortured during twenty-seven years of confinement in fifty different prisons, and was often deprived of the means of study and writing. After his release in 1626, he withdrew to France; and in 1639, died in a convent of his order. The *Civitas Solis seu idea reipublicae philosophicæ,* written in prison, is believed to have been the beginning of a large work, of which the first part was to deal with the laws of nature, the second with the manners and customs of men, the third with the organization of the state, the fourth with the economic bases of society. It was, as Campanella himself says, the counterpart of Plato's *Republic,* and on its scientific side was based on Telesius. It formulated for the first time a complete socialistic system on a scientific foundation,* and, in France especially, furnished a model for later ideal communities.

The city with its seven walls, its compact organization, its carefully divided labors, and rigorous discipline reflect the monastic experiences of the writer; but the principles, in accordance with which the state is governed, the social relation determined, and industry controlled, are such as to interest men in all ages. Collectively, the inhabitants labor for the common good; individually, each seeks the perfecting of his body and soul, the care of the young children, and the worship of God. Government is intrusted to the wisest and ablest, and laws are made and administered only so far as they promote the object for which all are laboring. The essences of life are equality, sacrifice of self for the community, the banishment of egotism; and peculiar features are the community of wives and goods, common meals, state control of produce, and of children after a certain age, dislike of commercial exchange, depreciation of money, love of all for manual labor, and the high regard which all show for intellectual and artistic pursuits. It is a remarkable fact

---

*Sigwart, *Kleine Schriften,* p. 151.

that in spite of Campanella's sufferings his work should not only show no trace of bitterness, but should maintain consistently the loftiest ideals.

Less purely Utopian in conception than the *City of the Sun* is Bacon's *Atlantis,* and almost entirely wanting is it in the communistic extravagances of Campanella's work. It contains an expression of the scientific views of Bacon and his opinion regarding the duty of the state toward science. More than this it describes his tastes in conduct and dress, and is characterized by a spirit of hospitality, kindliness, and courtesy, which betrays his sympathetic nature. As has been well said "there is no single work of his which has so much of himself in it." Unlike More, who would limit the population, Bacon, as the institutions of the Tirsan shows, would have families large; and unlike other writers of his age, he gives a prominent part and attractive character to Joabin, a Jew. But the chief interest of the author centers in Solomon's House, the College of the Six Days Works, a state institution governed by an official body, and founded for the purpose of discovering "the causes and secret motions of things." Here Bacon gives a list of those experiments and observations, which he hoped would increase knowledge, ameliorate the conditions of life, improve the physical well-being of man, and enlarge the bounds of the human empire. In medicine, surgery, meteorology, food, and mechanical contrivances he anticipates many of the improvements of later times. It has been generally supposed that "this noblest foundation that ever was on earth" suggested the foundation and program of the Royal Society in England and of similar societies abroad.

The systematic study of Utopias cannot but be fruitful of results. Fantastic though many of the systems are, each is nevertheless a mirror of the prevailing thought of the period in which it is written and a key to the ideals of the best men.

Charles M. Andrews.

BACON'S

NEW ATLANTIS.

NEW ATLANTIS.

WE SAILED from Peru, where we had continued by the space of one whole year, for China and Japan, by the South Sea, taking with us victuals for twelve months; and had good winds from the east, though soft and weak, for five months' space and more. But then the wind came about, and settled in the west for many days, so as we could make little or no way, and were sometimes in purpose to turn back. But then again there arose strong and great winds from the south, with a point east; which carried us up, for all that we could do, toward the north: by which time our victuals failed us, though we had made good spare of them. So that finding ourselves, in the midst of the greatest wilderness of waters in the world, without victual, we gave ourselves up for lost men, and prepared for death. Yet we did lift up our hearts and voices to God above, who showeth his wonders in the deep; beseeching him of his mercy, that as in the beginning he discovered the face of the deep, and brought forth dry land, so he would now discover land to us, that we might not perish. And it came to pass, that the next day about evening we saw within a kenning before us, toward the north, as it were, thick clouds which did put us in some hope of land: knowing how that part of the South Sea was utterly unknown; and might have islands or continents, that hitherto were not come to light. Wherefore we bent our course thither, where we saw the appearance of land, all that night; and in the dawning of next day, we might plainly discern that it was a land flat to our sight, and full of boscage, which made it show the more dark. And after an hour and a half's sailing we entered into a good haven, being the port of a fair city. Not great indeed, but well built, and that gave a pleasant view from the sea. And we thinking every minute long till we were on land, came close to the shore and offered to land. But straightway we saw divers of the people, with bastons in their hands, as it were, forbidding us to land: yet without any cries or fierceness, but only as warning us off, by signs that they made. Whereupon being not a little discomfited, we were advising with ourselves what we should do. During which time there made forth to us a small boat, with about eight persons in it, whereof one of them had in his hand a tipstaff of a yellow cane, tipped at both ends with blue, who made aboard our ship, without any show of distrust at all. And when he saw one of our number present himself somewhat afore the rest, he drew forth a little scroll of parchment (somewhat yellower than our parchment, and shining like the leaves of writing tables, but otherwise soft and flexible), and delivered it to our foremost man. In which scroll were written in ancient Hebrew, and in ancient Greek, and in good Latin of the school, and in Spanish these words: "Land ye not, none of you, and provide to be gone from this coast within sixteen days, except you have further time given you; meanwhile, if you want fresh water, or victual, or help for your sick, or that your ship needeth repair, write down your wants, and you shall have that which belongeth to mercy." This scroll was signed with a stamp of cherubim's wings, not spread, but hanging downward, and by them a cross. This being delivered, the officer returned, and left only a servant with us to receive our answer. Consulting hereupon among ourselves, we were much perplexed. The denial of landing, and hasty warning us away, troubled us much: on the other side, to find that the people had languages, and were so full of humanity, did comfort us not a little. And above all, the sign of the cross to that instrument, was to us a great rejoicing, and as it were a certain presage of good. Our answer was in the Spanish tongue, "That for our ship, it was well; for we had rather met with calms and contrary winds, than any tempests. For our sick, they were many, and in very ill case; so that if they were not permitted to land, they ran in danger of their lives." Our other wants we set down in particular, adding, "That we had some little store of merchandise, which if it pleased them to deal for, it might supply our wants, without being chargeable unto them." We offered some reward in pistolets unto the servant, and a piece of crimson velvet to be presented to the officer; but the servant took them not, nor would scarce look upon them; and so left us, and went back in another little boat which was sent for him.

About three hours after we had dispatched our answer there came toward us a person (as it seemed) of a place. He had on him a gown with wide sleeves, of a kind of water chamolet, of an excellent azure color, far more glossy than ours: his under apparel was green, and so was his hat, being in the form of a turban, daintily made, and not so huge as the Turkish turbans; and the locks of his hair came down below the brims of it. A reverend man was he to behold. He came in a boat, gilt in some part of it, with four persons more only in that boat; and was followed by another boat, wherein were some twenty. When he was come within a flight-shot of our ship, signs were made to us that we should send forth some to meet him upon the water, which we presently did in our ship-boat, sending the principal man among us save one, and four of our number with him. When we were come within six yards of their boat, they called to us to stay, and not to approach further, which we did. And thereupon the man, whom I before described, stood up, and with a loud voice in Spanish, asked, "Are ye Christians?" We answered, "We were;" fearing the less, because of the cross we had seen in the subscription. At which answer the said person lift up his right hand toward heaven, and drew it softly to his mouth (which is the gesture they use, when they thank God), and then said: "If ye will swear, all of you, by the merits of the Savior, that ye are no pirates; nor have shed blood, lawfully nor unlawfully, within forty days past; you may have license to come on land." We said, "We were all ready to take that oath." Whereupon one of those that were with him, being (as it seemed) a notary, made an entry of this act. Which done, another of the attendants of the great person, which was with him in the same boat, after his lord had spoken a little to him, said aloud: "My lord would have you know, that it is not of pride, or greatness, that he cometh not aboard your ship: but for that, in your answer, you declare that you have many sick among you, he was warned by the conservator of health of the city that he should keep a distance." We bowed ourselves toward him, and answered: "We were his humble servants; and accounted for great honor and singular humanity toward us, that which was already done: but hoped well, that the nature of the sickness of our men was not infectious." So he returned; and a while after came the notary to us aboard our ship; holding in his hand a fruit of that country, like an orange, but of color between orange-tawny and scarlet: which cast a most excellent odor. He used it (as it seemed) for a preservative against infection. He gave us our oath, "By the name of Jesus, and his merits:" and after told us, that the next day by six of the clock in the morning, we should be sent to, and brought to the strangers' house (so he called it), where we should be accommodated of things, both for our whole and for our sick. So he left us; and when we offered him some pistolets, he smiling, said, "He must not be twice paid for one labor:" meaning (as I take it) that he had salary sufficient of the state for his service. For (as I after learned) they call an officer that taketh rewards twice paid.

The next morning early, there came to us the same officer that came to us at first with his cane, and told us: "He came to conduct us to the strangers' house: and that he had prevented the hour, because we might have the whole day before us for our business. For (said he) if you will follow my advice, there shall first go with me some few of you, and see the place, and how it may be made convenient for you: and then you may send for your sick and the rest of your number, which ye will bring on land." We thanked him, and said, "That his care which he took of desolate strangers, God would reward." And so six of us went on land with him; and when we were on land, he went before us, and turned to us and said, "He was but our servant and our guide." He led us through three fair streets; and all the way we went there were gathered some people on both sides, standing in a row; but in so civil a fashion, as if it had been, not to wonder at us, but to welcome us; and divers of them, as we passed by them, put their arms a little abroad, which is their gesture when they bid any welcome. The strangers' house is a fair and spacious house, built of brick, of somewhat a bluer color than our brick; and with handsome windows, some of glass, some of a kind of cambric oiled. He brought us first into a fair parlor above stairs, and then asked us, "What number of persons we were? and how many sick?" We answered, "We were in all (sick and whole) one and fifty persons, whereof our sick were seventeen." He desired us to have patience a little, and to stay till he came back to us which was about an hour after; and then he led us to see the chambers which were provided for us, being in number nineteen. They having cast it (as it seemeth) that four of those chambers, which were better than the rest, might receive four of the principal men of our company; and lodge them alone by themselves; and the other fifteen chambers were to lodge us, two and two together. The chambers were handsome and cheerful chambers, and furnished civilly. Then he led us to a long gallery like a dorture, where he showed us all along the one side (for the other side was but wall and window) seventeen cells, very neat ones, having partitions of cedar wood. Which gallery and cells, being in all forty (many more than we needed), were instituted as an infirmary for sick persons. And he told us withal, that as any of our sick waxed well, he might be removed from his cell to a chamber: for which purpose there were set forth ten spare chambers, besides the number we spake of before. This done, he brought us back to the parlor, and lifting up his cane a little (as they do when they give and charge or command), said to us, "Ye are to know that the custom of the land requireth, that after this day and to-morrow (which we give you for removing your people from your ship), you are to keep within doors for three days. But let it not trouble you, nor do not think yourselves restrained, but rather left to your rest and ease. You shall want nothing; and there are six of our people appointed to attend you for any business you may have abroad." We gave him thanks with all affection and respect, and said, "God surely is manifested in this land." We offered him also twenty pistolets, but he smiled and only said: "What? Twice paid!" And so he left us. Soon after our dinner was served; in which was right good viands, both for bread and meat; better than any collegiate diet that I have known in Europe. We had also drink of three sorts, all wholesome and good; wine of the grape; a drink of grain, such as is with us our ale, but more clear; and a kind of cider made of a fruit of that country; a wonderful pleasing and refreshing drink. Besides, there were brought in to us great store of those scarlet oranges for our sick; which (they said) were an assured remedy for sickness taken at sea. There was given us also a box of small grey or whitish pills, which they wished our sick should take, one of the pills every night before sleep; which (they said) would hasten their recovery. The next day, after that our trouble of carriage and removing of our men and goods out of our ship was somewhat settled and quiet, I thought good to call our company together, and when they were assembled, said unto them, "My dear friends, let us know ourselves, and how it standeth with us. We are men cast on land, as Jonas was out of the whale's belly, when we were as buried in the deep; and now we are on land, we are but between death and life, for we are beyond both the old world and the new; and whether ever we shall see Europe, God only knoweth. It is a kind of miracle hath brought us hither, and it must be little less that shall bring us hence. Therefore in regard of our deliverance past, and our danger present and to come, let us look up to God, and every man reform his own ways. Besides we are come here among a Christian people, full of piety and humanity. Let us not bring that confusion of face upon ourselves, as to show our vices or unworthiness before them. Yet there is more, for they have by commandment (though in form of courtesy) cloistered us within these walls for three days; who knoweth whether it be not to take some taste of our manners and conditions? And if they find them bad, to banish us straightway; if good, to give us further time. For these men that they have given us for attendance, may withal have an eye upon us. Therefore, for God's love, and as we love the weal of our souls and bodies, let us so behave ourselves, as we may be at peace with God, and may find grace in the eyes of this people." Our company with one voice thanked me for my good admonition, and promised me to live soberly and civilly, and without giving any the least occasion of offense. So we spent our three days joyfully, and without care, in expectation what would be done with us when they were expired. During which time, we had every hour joy of the amendment of our sick, who thought themselves cast into some divine pool of healing, they mended so kindly and so fast.

The morrow after our three days were past, there came to us a new man, that we had not seen before, clothed in blue as the former was, save that his turban was white with a small red cross on the top. He had also a tippet of fine linen. At his coming in, he did bend to us a little, and put his arms abroad. We of our parts saluted him in a very lowly and submissive manner; as looking that from him we should receive sentence of life or death. He desired to speak with some few of us. Whereupon six of us only stayed, and the rest avoided the room. He said, " I am by office governor of this house of strangers, and by vocation I am a Christian priest; and therefore am come to you, to offer you my service, both as strangers, and chiefly as Christians. Some things I may tell you, which I think you will not be unwilling to hear. The state hath given you license to stay on land for the space of six weeks : and let it not trouble you, if your occasions ask further time, for the law in this point is not precise; and I do not doubt, but myself shall be able to obtain for you such further time as shall be convenient. Ye shall also understand, that the strangers' house is at this time rich, and much afore-hand; for it hath laid up revenue these thirty-seven years; for so long it is since any stranger arrived in this part; and therefore take ye no care; the state will defray you all the time you stay. Neither shall you stay one day the less for that. As for any merchandise you have brought, ye shall be well used, and have your return, either in merchandise or in gold and silver; for to us it is all one. And if you have any other request to make, hide it not; for ye shall find we will not make your countenance to fall by the answer ye shall receive. Only this I must tell you, that none of you must go above a karan (that is with them a mile and a half) from the walls of the city, without special leave." We answered, after we had looked a while upon one another, admiring this gracious and parent-like usage, that we could not tell what to say, for we wanted words to express our thanks; and his noble, free offers left us nothing to ask. It seemed to us, that we had before us a picture of our salvation in heaven; for we that were a while since in the jaws of death, were now brought into a place where we found nothing but consolations. For the commandment laid upon us, we would not fail to obey it, though it was impossible but our hearts should be inflamed to tread further upon this happy and holy ground. We added, that our tongues should first cleave to the roofs of our mouths, ere we should forget, either this reverend person, or this whole nation, in our prayers. We also most humbly besought him to accept of us as his true servants, by as just a right as ever men on earth were bounden; laying and presenting both our persons and all we had at his feet. He said, he was a priest and looked for a priest's reward; which was our brotherly love, and the good of our souls and bodies. So he went from us, not without tears of tenderness in his eyes, and left us also confused with joy and kindness, saying among ourselves, that we were come into a land of angels, which did appear to us daily and present us with comforts, which we thought not of, much less expected.

The next day, about ten of the clock, the governor came to us again, and after salutations, said familiarly, that he was come to visit us; and called for a chair, and sat him down; and we being some ten of us (the rest were of the meaner sort, or else gone abroad), sat down with him; and when we were set, he began thus: "We of this island of Bensalem (for so they called it in their

language) have this: that by means of our solitary situation, and of the laws of secrecy, which we have for our
travelers, and our rare admission of strangers; we know
well most part of the habitable world, and are ourselves
unknown. Therefore because he that knoweth least is
fittest to ask questions, it is more reason, for the enter-
tainment of the time, that ye ask me questions, than that
I ask you." We answered, that we humbly thanked him,
that he would give us leave so to do. And that we conceived by the taste we had already, that there was no
worldly thing on earth more worthy to be known than
the state of that happy land. But above all (we said)
since that we were met from the several ends of the
world, and hoped assuredly that we should meet one day
in the kingdom of heaven (for that we were both parts
Christians), we desired to know (in respect that land was
so remote, and so divided by vast and unknown seas
from the land where our Savior walked on earth) who
was the apostle of that nation, and how it was converted to the faith ? It appeared in his face, that he took
great contentment in this our question; he said, "Ye
knit my heart to you, by asking this question in the
first place: for it showeth that you first seek the kingdom of heaven: and I shall gladly, and briefly, satisfy
your demand.

"About twenty years after the ascension of our Savior
it came to pass, that there was seen by the people of
Renfusa (a city upon the eastern coast of our island,
within sight, the night was cloudy and calm), as it might
be some mile in the sea, a great pillar of light; not
sharp, but in form of a column, or cylinder, rising from
the sea, a great way up toward heaven; and on the top
of it was seen a large cross of light, more bright and
resplendent than the body of the pillar. Upon which so
strange a spectacle, the people of the city gathered apace
together upon the sands, to wonder; and so after put
themselves into a number of small boats to go nearer to
this marvelous sight. But when the boats were come
within about sixty yards of the pillar, they found themselves all bound, and could go no further, yet so as they
might move to go about, but might not approach nearer;

so as the boats stood all as in a theater, beholding this light, as an heavenly sign. It so fell out, that there was in one of the boats one of the wise men of the Society of Salomon's House; which house or college, my good brethren, is the very eye of this kingdom, who having a while attentively and devoutly viewed and contemplated this pillar and cross, fell down upon his face; and then raised himself upon his knees, and lifting up his hands to heaven, made his prayers in this manner:

"'Lord God of heaven and earth; thou hast vouchsafed of thy grace, to those of our order to know thy works of creation, and true secrets of them; and to discern (as far as appertaineth to the generations of men) between divine miracles, works of Nature, works of art and. impostures, and illusions of all sorts. I do here acknowledge and testify before this people, that the thing we now see before our eyes, is thy finger, and a true miracle. And forasmuch as we learn in our books, that thou never workest miracles, but to a divine and excellent end (for the laws of Nature are thine own laws, and thou exceedest them not but upon great cause), we most humbly beseech thee to prosper this great sign, and to give us the interpretation and use of it in mercy; which thou dost in some part secretly promise, by sending it unto us.'

"When he had made his prayer, he presently found the boat he was in movable and unbound; whereas all the rest remained still fast; and taking that for an assurance of leave to approach, he caused the boat to be softly and with silence rowed toward the pillar; but ere he came near it, the pillar and cross of light broke up, and cast itself abroad, as it were into a firmament of many stars, which also vanished soon after, and there was nothing left to be seen but a small ark, or chest of cedar, dry and not wet at all with water, though it swam; and in the fore end of it, which was toward him, grew a small green branch of palm; and when the wise man had taken it with all reverence into his boat, it opened of itself, and there were found in it a book and a letter, both written in fine parchment, and wrapped in sindons of linen. The book contained all the canonical books of the Old and

New Testament, according as you have them (for we know well what the churches with you receive), and the Apocalypse itself; and some other books of the New Testament, which were not at that time written, were nevertheless in the book. And for the letter, it was in these words:

" 'I Bartholomew, a servant of the Highest, and apostle of Jesus Christ, was warned by an angel that appeared to me in a vision of glory, that I should commit this ark to the floods of the sea. Therefore I do testify and declare unto that people where God shall ordain this ark to come to land, that in the same day is come unto them salvation and peace, and good will from the Father, and from the Lord Jesus.'

" There was also in both these writings, as well the book as the letter, wrought a great miracle, conform to that of the apostles, in the original gift of tongues. For there being at that time, in this land, Hebrews, Persians, and Indians, besides the natives, every one read upon the book and letter, as if they had been written in his own language. And thus was this land saved from infidelity (as the remain of the old world was from water) by an ark, through the apostolical and miraculous evangelism of St. Bartholomew." And here he paused, and a messenger came, and called him forth from us. So this was all that passed in that conference.

The next day, the same governor came again to us, immediately after dinner, and excused himself, saying, " That the day before he was called from us somewhat abruptly, but now he would make us amends, and spend time with us, if we held his company and conference agreeable." We answered, that we held it so agreeable and pleasing to us, as we forgot both dangers past, and fears to come, for the time we heard him speak; and that we thought an hour spent with him was worth years of our former life. He bowed himself a little to us, and after we were set again, he said, " Well, the questions are on your part." One of our number said, after a little pause, that there was a matter we were no less desirous to know than fearful to ask, lest we might presume too far. But encouraged by his rare humanity toward us (that could scarce think ourselves strangers, being his vowed and professed servants), we would take the hardness to propound it; humbly beseeching him, if he thought it not fit to be answered, that he would pardon it, though he rejected it. We said, we well observed those his words, which he formerly spake, that this happy island, where we now stood, was known to few, and yet knew most of the nations of the world, which we found to be true, considering they had the languages of Europe, and knew much of our state and business; and yet we in Europe (notwithstanding all the remote discoveries and navigations of this last age) never heard any of the least inkling or glimpse of this island. This we found wonderful strange; for that all nations have interknowledge one of another, either by voyage into foreign parts, or by strangers that come to them; and though the traveler into a foreign country doth commonly know more by the eye than he that stayeth at home can by relation of the traveler: yet both ways suffice to make a mutual knowledge, in some degree, on both parts. But for this island, we never heard tell of any ship of theirs, that had been seen to arrive upon any shore of Europe; no, nor of either the East or West Indies, nor yet of any ship of any other part of the world, that had made return for them. And yet the marvel rested not in this. For the situation of it (as his lordship said) in the secret conclave of such a vast sea might cause it. But then, that they should have knowledge of the languages, books, affairs, of those that lie such a distance from them, it was a thing we could not tell what to make of; for that it seemed to us a condition and propriety of divine powers and beings, to be hidden and unseen to others, and yet to have others open, and as in a light to them. At this speech the governor gave a gracious smile and said, that we did well to ask pardon for this question we now asked, for that it imported, as if we thought this land a land of magicians, that sent forth spirits of the air into all parts, to bring them news and intelligence of other countries. It was answered by us all, in all possible humbleness, but yet with a countenance taking knowledge, that we knew that he spake it but merrily. That we were apt enough to think, there was somewhat supernatural in this island, but yet rather as angelical than magical. But to let his lordship know truly what it was that made us tender and doubtful to ask this question, it was not any such conceit, but because we remembered he had given a touch in his former speech, that this land had laws of secrecy touching strangers. To this he said, "You remember it aright; and therefore in that I shall say to you, I must reserve some particulars, which it is not lawful for me to reveal, but there will be enough left to give you satisfaction.

"You shall understand (that which perhaps you will scarce think credible) that about three thousand years ago, or somewhat more, the navigation of the world (especially for remote voyages) was greater than at this day. Do not think with yourselves, that I know not how much it is increased with you, within these threescore years; I know it well, and yet I say, greater then than now; whether it was, that the example of the ark, that saved the remnant of men from the universal deluge, gave men confidence to adventure upon the waters, or what it was; but such is the truth. The Phœnicians, and especially the Tyrians, had great fleets; so had the Carthaginians their colony, which is yet farther west. Toward the east the shipping of Egypt, and of Palestine, was likewise great. China also, and the great Atlantis (that you call America), which have now but junks and canoes, abounded then in tall ships. This island (as appeareth by faithful registers of those times) had then fifteen hundred strong ships, of great content. Of all this there is with you sparing memory, or none; but we have large knowledge thereof.

"At that time, this land was known and frequented by the ships and vessels of all the nations before named. And (as it cometh to pass) they had many times men of other countries, that were no sailors, that came with them; as Persians, Chaldeans, Arabians, so as almost all nations of might and fame resorted hither; of whom we have some stirps and little tribes with us at this day. And for our own ships, they went sundry voyages, as well to your straits, which you call the Pillars of Hercules, as to other parts in the Atlantic and Mediterranean Seas; as to Paguin (which is the same with Cambalaine) and Quinzy, upon the Oriental Seas, as far as to the borders of the East Tartary.

"At the same time, and an age after or more, the inhabitants of the great Atlantis did flourish. For though the narration and description which is made by a great man with you, that the descendants of Neptune planted there, and of the magnificent temple, palace, city and hill; and the manifold streams of goodly navigable rivers, which as so many chains environed the same site and temple; and the several degrees of ascent, whereby men did climb up to the same, as if it had been a Scala Cœli; be all poetical and fabulous; yet so much is true, that the said country of Atlantis, as well as that of Peru, then called Coya, as that of Mexico, then named Tyrambel, were mighty and proud kingdoms, in arms, shipping, and riches; so mighty, as at one time, or at least within the space of ten years, they both made two great expeditions: they of Tyrambel through the Atlantic to the Mediterranean Sea; and they of Coya, through the South Sea upon this our island; and for the former of these, which was into Europe, the same author among you, as it seemeth, had some relation from the Egyptian priest, whom he citeth. For assuredly, such a thing there was. But whether it were the ancient Athenians that had the glory of the repulse and resistance of those forces, I can say nothing; but certain it is there never came back either ship or man from that voyage. Neither had the other voyage of those of Coya upon us had better fortune, if they had not met with enemies of greater clemency. For the king of this island, by name Altabin, a wise man and a great warrior, knowing well both his own strength and that of his enemies, handled the matter so, as he cut off their land forces from their ships, and entoiled both their navy and their camp with a greater power than theirs, both by sea and land; and compelled them to render themselves without striking a stroke; and after they were at his mercy, contenting himself only with their oath, that they should no more bear arms against him, dismissed them all in safety. But the divine revenge overtook not long after those proud enterprises. For within less than the space of one hundred years the Great Atlantis was utterly lost and destroyed; not by a great earthquake, as your man saith, for that whole tract is little subject to earthquakes, but by a particular deluge, or inundation; those countries having at this day far greater rivers, and far higher mountains, to pour down waters, than any part of the old world. But it is true that the same inundation was not deep, not past forty foot, in most places, from the ground, so that although it destroyed man and beast generally, yet some few wild inhabitants of the wood escaped. Birds also were saved by flying to the high trees and woods. For as for men, although they had buildings in many places higher than the depth of the water, yet that inundation, though it were shallow, had a long continuance, whereby they of the vale that were not drowned perished for want of food and other things necessary. So as marvel you not at the thin population of America, nor at the rudeness and ignorance of the people; for you must account your inhabitants of America as a young people, younger a thousand years at the least than the rest of the world, for that there was so much time between the universal flood and their particular inundation. For the poor remnant of human seed which remained in their mountains, peopled the country again slowly, by little and little, and being simple and a savage people (not like Noah and his sons, which was the chief family of the earth), they were not able to leave letters, arts, and civility to their posterity; and having likewise in their mountainous habitations been used, in respect of the extreme cold of those regions, to clothe themselves with the skins of tigers, bears, and great hairy goats, that they have in those parts; when after they came down into the valley, and found the intolerable heats which are there, and knew no means of lighter apparel, they were forced to begin the custom of going naked, which continueth at this day. Only they take great pride and delight in the feathers of birds, and this also they took from those their ancestors of the mountains, who were invited unto it, by the infinite flight of birds, that came up to the high grounds, while the waters stood below. So you see, by this main accident of time, we lost our traffic with the Americans, with whom of all others, in regard they lay nearest to us, we had most commerce. As for the other parts of the world, it is most manifest that in the ages following (whether it were in respect of wars, or by a natural revolution of time) navigation did everywhere greatly decay, and specially far voyages (the rather by the use of galleys, and such vessels as could hardly brook the ocean) were altogether left and omitted. So then, that part of intercourse which could be from other nations, to sail to us, you see how it hath long since ceased; except it were by some rare accident, as this of yours. But now of the cessation of that other part of intercourse, which might be by our sailing to other nations, I must yield you some other cause. For I cannot say, if I shall say truly, but our shipping for number, strength, mariners, pilots, and all things that appertain to navigation, is as great as ever; and therefore why we should sit at home, I shall now give you an account by itself; and it will draw nearer, to give you satisfaction, to your principal question.

" There reigned in this island, about 1,900 years ago, a king, whose memory of all others we most adore; not superstitiously, but as a divine instrument, though a mortal man: his name was Salomona; and we esteem him as the lawgiver of our nation. This king had a large heart, inscrutable for good; and was wholly bent to make his kingdom and people happy. He therefore taking into consideration how sufficient and substantive this land was, to maintain itself without any aid at all of the foreigner; being 5,000 miles in circuit, and of rare fertility of soil, in the greatest part thereof; and finding also the shipping of this country might be plentifully set on work, both by fishing and by transportations from port to port, and likewise by sailing unto some small islands that are not far from us, and are under the crown and laws of this state; and recalling into his memory the happy and flourishing estate wherein this land then was, so as it might be a thousand ways altered to the worse, but scarce any one way to the better; though nothing wanted to his noble and heroical intentions, but only (as far as human foresight might reach) to give perpetuity to that which was in his time so happily established, therefore among his other fundamental laws of this kingdom he did ordain the interdicts and prohibitions which we have touching entrance of strangers; which at that time (though it was after the calamity of America) was frequent; doubting novelties and commixture of manners. It is true, the like law against the admission of strangers without license is an ancient law in the kingdom of China, and yet continued in use. But there it is a poor thing; and hath made them a curious, ignorant, fearful foolish nation. But our lawgiver made his law of another temper. For first, he hath preserved all points of humanity, in taking order and making provision for the relief of strangers distressed; whereof you have tasted." At which speech (as reason was) we all rose up, and bowed ourselves He went on: "That king also still desiring to join humanity and policy together; and thinking it against humanity, to detain strangers here against their wills; and against policy, that they should return, and discover their knowledge of this estate, he took this course; he did ordain, that of the strangers that should be permitted to land, as many at all times might depart as many as would; but as many as would stay, should have very good conditions, and means to live from the state. Wherein he saw so far, that now in so many ages since the prohibition, we have memory not of one ship that ever returned, and but of thirteen persons only, at several times, that chose to return in our bottoms. What those few that returned may have reported abroad, I know not. But you must think, whatsoever they have said, could be taken where they came but for a dream. Now for our traveling from hence into parts abroad, our lawgiver thought fit altogether to restrain it. So is it not in China. For the Chinese sail where they will, or can; which showeth, that their law of keeping out strangers is a law of pusillanimity and fear. But this restraint of ours hath one only exception, which is admirable; preserving the good which cometh by communi-

cating with strangers, and avoiding the hurt: and I will
now open it to you. And here I shall seem a little to
digress, but you will by-and-by find it pertinent. Ye
shall understand, my dear friends, that among the
excellent acts of that king, one above all hath the pre-
eminence. It was the erection and institution of an
order, or society, which we call Salomon's House; the
noblest foundation, as we think, that ever was upon the
earth, and the lantern of this kingdom. It is dedicated
to the study of the works and creatures of God. Some
think it beareth the founder's name a little corrupted,
as if it should be Solomon's House. But the records
write it as it is spoken. So as I take it to be de-
nominate of the king of the Hebrews, which is famous
with you and no strangers to us; for we have some parts of
his works which with you are lost; namely, that natural
history which he wrote of all plants, from the cedar of
Libanus to the moss that groweth out of the wall; and of
all things that have life and motion. This maketh me
think that our king finding himself to symbolize, in many
things, with that king of the Hebrews, which lived many
years before him, honored him with the title of this foundation. And I am the rather induced to be of this opinion,
for that I find in ancient records, this order or society is
sometimes called Solomon's House, and sometimes the
College of the Six Days' Works; whereby I am satisfied
that our excellent king had learned from the Hebrews
that God had created the world, and all that therein is,
within six days: and therefore he instituted that house,
for the finding out of the true nature of all things,
whereby God might have the more glory in the work-
manship of them, and men the more fruit in their use of
them, did give it also that second name. But now to
come to our present purpose. When the king had forbidden to all his people navigation into any part that was
not under his crown, he made, nevertheless, this ordinance;
that every twelve years there should be set forth out of
this kingdom, two ships, appointed to several voyages;
that in either of these ships there should be a mission of
three of the fellows or brethren of Salomon's House,
whose errand was only to give us knowledge of the affairs

and state of those countries to which they were designed;
and especially of the sciences, arts, manufactures, and
inventions of all the world; and withal to bring unto us
books, instruments, and patterns in every kind: that the
ships, after they had landed the brethren, should return;
and that the brethren should stay abroad till the new
mission, the ships are not otherwise fraught than with
store of victuals, and good quantity of treasure to remain
with the brethren, for the buying of such things, and
rewarding of such persons, as they should think fit. Now
for me to tell you how the vulgar sort of mariners are
contained from being discovered at land, and how they
that must be put on shore for any time, color themselves
under the names of other nations, and to what places
these voyages have been designed; and what places of
rendezvous are appointed for the new missions, and the
like circumstances of the practice, I may not do it, neither
is it much to your desire. But thus you see we maintain a
trade, not for gold, silver, or jewels, nor for silks, nor
for spices, nor any other commodity of matter; but only
for God's first creature, which was light; to have light, I
say, of the growth of all parts of the world." And when
he had said this, he was silent, and so were we all; for
indeed we were all astonished to hear so strange things
so probably told. And he perceiving that we were willing
to say somewhat, but had it not ready, in great courtesy
took us off, and descended to ask us questions of our
voyage and fortunes, and in the end concluded that we
might do well to think with ourselves, what time of stay
we would demand of the state, and bade us not to scant
ourselves; for he would procure such time as we desired.
Whereupon we all rose up and presented ourselves to kiss
the skirt of his tippet, but he would not suffer us, and so
took his leave. But when it came once among our
people, that the state used to offer conditions to strangers
that would stay, we had work enough to get any of our
men to look to our ship, and to keep them from going
presently to the governor, to crave conditions; but with
much ado we restrained them, till we might agree what
course to take.

We took ourselves now for freemen, seeing there was

no danger of our utter perdition, and lived most joyfully,
going abroad and seeing what was to be seen in the city
and places adjacent, within our tedder; and obtaining
acquaintance with many of the city, not of the meanest
quality, at whose hands we found such humanity, and
such a freedom and desire to take strangers, as it were,
into their bosom, as was enough to make us forget all
that was dear to us in our own countries: and continually we met with many things, right worthy of observation and relation; as indeed, if there be a mirror in the
world, worthy to hold men's eyes, it is that country.
One day there were two of our company bidden to a
feast of the family, as they call it; a most natural, pious,
and reverend custom it is, showing that nation to be
compounded of all goodness. This is the manner of it:
it is granted to any man that shall live to see thirty
persons descended of his body, alive together, and all
above three years old, to make this feast, which is done
at the cost of the state. The father of the family, whom
they call the Tirsan, two days before the feast, taketh
to him three of such friends as he liketh to choose, and
is assisted also by the governor of the city or place where
the feast is celebrated, and all the persons of the family,
of both sexes, are summoned to attend him. These two
days the Tirsan sitteth in consultation, concerning the
good estate of the family. There, if there be any dis-
cord or suits between any of the family, they are compounded and appeased. There, if any of the family be
distressed or decayed, order is taken for their relief, and
competent means to live. There, if any be subject to
vice, or take ill courses, they are reproved and censured.
So likewise direction is given touching marriages, and
the courses of life which any of them should take, with
divers other the like orders and advices. The governor
assisteth to the end, to put into execution, by his public
authority, the decrees and orders of the Tirsan, if they
should be disobeyed, though that seldom needeth; such
reverence and obedience they give to the order of Nature.
The Tirsan doth also then ever choose one man from
among his sons, to live in house with him; who is
called ever after the Son of the Vine. The reason will

hereafter appear. On the feast day, the father or Tirsan cometh forth after divine service into a large room where the feast is celebrated; which room hath an half-pace at the upper end. Against the wall, in the middle of the half-pace, is a chair placed for him, with a table and carpet before it. Over the chair is a state, made round or oval, and it is of ivy; an ivy somewhat whiter than ours, like the leaf of a silver asp, but more shining; for it is green all winter. And the state is curiously wrought with silver and silk of divers colors, broiding or binding in the ivy; and is ever of the work of some of the daughters of the family; and veiled over at the top, with a fine net of silk and silver. But the substance of it is true ivy; whereof after it is taken down, the friends of the family are desirous to have some leaf or sprig to keep. The Tirsan cometh forth with all his generation or lineage, the males before him, and the females following him; and if there be a mother, from whose body the whole lineage is descended, there is a traverse placed in a loft above on the right hand of the chair, with a privy door, and a carved window of glass, leaded with gold and blue; where she sitteth, but is not seen. When the Tirsan is come forth, he sitteth down in the chair; and all the lineage place themselves against the wall, both at his back, and upon the return of the half-pace, in order of their years, without difference of sex, and stand upon their feet. When he is set, the room being always full of company, but well kept and without disorder, after some pause there cometh in from the lower end of the room a Taratan (which is as much as an herald), and on either side of him two young lads: whereof one carrieth a scroll of their shining yellow parchment, and the other a cluster of grapes of gold, with a long foot or stalk. The herald and children are clothed with mantles of sea-water green satin; but the herald's mantle is streamed with gold, and hath a train. Then the herald with three curtsies, or rather inclinations, cometh up as far as the half-pace, and there first taketh into his hand the scroll. This scroll is the king's charter, containing gift of revenue, and many privileges, exemptions, and points of honor, granted to the father of the family, and it is ever styled and directed, "To such an one, our well-beloved friend and creditor," which is a title proper only to this case. For they say, the king is debtor to no man, but for propagation of his subjects; the seal set to the king's charter is the king's image, embossed or molded in gold; and though such charters be expedited of course, and as of right, yet they are varied by discretion, according to the number and dignity of the family. This charter the herald readeth aloud; and while it is read, the father or Tirsan standeth up, supported by two of his sons, such as he chooseth. Then the herald mounteth the half-pace, and delivereth the charter into his hand: and with that there is an acclamation, by all that are present, in their language, which is thus much, "Happy are the people of Bensalem." Then the herald taketh into his hand from the other child the cluster of grapes, which is of gold; both the stalk, and the grapes. But the grapes are daintily enameled; and if the males of the family be the greater number, the grapes are enameled purple, with a little sun set on the top; if the females, then they are enameled into a greenish yellow, with a crescent on the top. The grapes are in number as many as there are descendants of the family. This golden cluster the herald delivereth also to the Tirsan; who presently delivereth it over to that son that he had formerly chosen, to be in house with him; who beareth it before his father, as an ensign of honor, when he goeth in public ever after; and is thereupon called the Son of the Vine. After this ceremony endeth the father or Tirsan retireth; and after some time cometh forth again to dinner, where he sitteth alone under the state, as before; and none of his descendants sit with him, of what degree or dignity so ever, except he hap to be of Salomon's House. He is served only by his own children, such as are male; who perform unto him all service of the table upon the knee, and the women only stand about him, leaning against the wall. The room below his half-pace hath tables on the sides for the guests that are bidden; who are served with great and comely order; and toward the end of dinner (which in the greatest feasts with them lasteth never above an hour and a half) there

is an hymn sung, varied according to the invention of
him that composeth it (for they have excellent poesy),
but the subject of it is always the praises of Adam, and
Noah, and Abraham; whereof the former two peopled the
world, and the last was the father of the faithful: con-
cluding ever with a thanksgiving for the nativity of our
Savior, in whose birth the births of all are only blessed.
Dinner being done, the Tirsan retireth again; and having
withdrawn himself alone into a place, where he maketh
some private prayers, he cometh forth the third time, to
give the blessing; with all his descendants, who stand
about him as at the first. Then he calleth them forth by
one and by one, by name as he pleaseth, though seldom
the order of age be inverted. The person that is called
(the table being before removed) kneeleth down before the
chair, and the father layeth his hand upon his head, or
her head, and giveth the blessing in these words: "Son
of Bensalem (or daughter of Bensalem), thy father saith
it; the man by whom thou hast breath and life speaketh
the word; the blessing of the everlasting Father, the
Prince of Peace, and the Holy Dove be upon thee, and
make the days of thy pilgrimage good and many." This
he saith to every of them; and that done, if there be
any of his sons of eminent merit and virtue, so they be
not above two, he calleth for them again, and saith,
laying his arm over their shoulders, they standing: "Sons,
it is well you are born, give God the praise, and perse-
vere to the end." And withal delivereth to either of
them a jewel, made in the figure of an ear of wheat,
which they ever after wear in the front of their turban,
or hat; this done, they fall to music and dances, and
other recreations, after their manner, for the rest of the
day. This is the full order of that feast.

By that time six or seven days were spent, I was fallen
into straight acquaintance with a merchant of that city,
whose name was Joabin. He was a Jew and circumcised;
for they have some few stirps of Jews yet remaining
among them, whom they leave to their own religion.
Which they may the better do, because they are of a
far differing disposition from the Jews in other parts.
For whereas they hate the name of Christ, and have a

secret inbred rancor against the people among whom they live; these, contrariwise, give unto our Savior many high attributes, and love the nation of Bensalem extremely. Surely this man of whom I speak would ever acknowledge that Christ was born of a Virgin; and that he was more than a man; and he would tell how God made him ruler of the seraphims, which guard his throne; and they call him also the Milken Way, and the Eliah of the Messiah, and many other high names, which though they be inferior to his divine majesty, yet they are far from the language of other Jews. And for the country of Bensalem, this man would make no end of commending it, being desirous by tradition among the Jews there to have it believed that the people thereof were of the generations of Abraham, by another son, whom they call Nachoran; and that Moses by a secret cabala ordained the laws of Bensalem which they now use; and that when the Messias should come, and sit in his throne at Hierusalem, the King of Bensalem should sit at his feet, whereas other kings should keep a great distance. But yet setting aside these Jewish dreams, the man was a wise man and learned, and of great policy, and excellently seen in the laws and customs of that nation. Among other discourses one day I told him, I was much affected with the relation I had from some of the company of their custom in holding the feast of the family, for that, methought, I had never heard of a solemnity wherein Nature did so much preside. And because propagation of families proceedeth from the nuptial copulation, I desired to know of him what laws and customs they had concerning marriage, and whether they kept marriage well, and whether they were tied to one wife? For that where population is so much affected, and such as with them it seemed to be, there is commonly permission of plurality of wives. To this he said: "You have reason for to commend that excellent institution of the feast of the family; and indeed we have experience, that those families that are partakers of the blessings of that feast, do flourish and prosper ever after, in an extraordinary manner. But hear me now, and I will tell you what I know. You shall understand that there is not under the heavens so chaste a nation as this of Bensalem, nor so free from all pollution or foulness. It is the virgin of the world; I remember, I have read in one of your European books, of an holy hermit among you, that desired to see the spirit of fornication, and there appeared to him a little foul ugly Ethiope; but if he had desired to see the spirit of chastity of Bensalem, it would have appeared to him in the likeness of a fair beautiful cherubim. For there is nothing, among mortal men, more fair and admirable than the chaste minds of this people. Know, therefore, that with them there are no stews, no dissolute houses, no courtesans, nor anything of that kind. Nay, they wonder, with detestation, at you in Europe, which permit such things. They say ye have put marriage out of office; for marriage is ordained a remedy for unlawful concupiscence; and natural concupiscence seemeth as a spur to marriage. But when men have at hand a remedy, more agreeable to their corrupt will, marriage is almost expulsed. And therefore there are with you seen infinite men that marry not, but choose rather a libertine and impure single life, than to be yoked in marriage; and many that do marry, marry late, when the prime and strength of their years is past. And when they do marry, what is marriage to them but a very bargain; wherein is sought alliance, or portion, or reputation, with some desire (almost indifferent) of issue; and not the faithful nuptial union of man and wife, that was first instituted. Neither is it possible that those that have cast away so basely so much of their strength, should greatly esteem children (being of the same matter) as chaste men do. So likewise during marriage is the case much amended, as it ought to be if those things were tolerated only for necessity; no, but they remain still as a very affront to marriage. The haunting of those dissolute places, or resort to courtesans, are no more punished in married men than in bachelors. And the depraved custom of change, and the delight in meretricious embracements (where sin is turned into art), maketh marriage a dull thing, and a kind of imposition or tax. They hear you defend these things, as done to avoid greater evils; as advoutries, deflowering of virgins, unnatural lust, and the like. But they say, this is a preposterous wisdom; and they call it Lot's offer, who to save his guests from abusing, offered his daughters; nay, they say further, that there is little gained in this; for that the same vices and appetites do still remain and abound, unlawful lust being like a furnace, that if you stop the flames altogether it will quench, but if you give it any vent it will rage; as for masculine love, they have no touch of it; and yet there are not so faithful and inviolate friendships in the world again as are there, and to speak generally (as I said before) I have not read of any such chastity in any people as theirs. And their usual saying is that whosoever is unchaste cannot reverence himself; and they say that the reverence of a man's self, is, next religion, the chiefest bridle of all vices.» And when he had said this the good Jew paused a little; whereupon I, far more willing to hear him speak on than to speak myself; yet thinking it decent that upon his pause of speech I should not be altogether silent, said only this; that I would say to him, as the widow of Sarepta said to Elias: «that he was come to bring to memory our sins»; and that I confess the righteousness of Bensalem was greater than the righteousness of Europe. At which speech he bowed his head and went on in this manner: " They have also many wise and excellent laws touching marriage. They allow no polygamy. They have ordained that none do intermarry, or contract, until a month be passed from their first interview. Marriage without consent of parents they do not make void, but they mulct it in the inheritors; for the children of such marriages are not admitted to inherit above a third part of their parents' inheritance. I have read in a book of one of your men, of a feigned commonwealth, where the married couple are permitted, before they contract, to see one another naked. This they dislike; for they think it a scorn to give a refusal after so familiar knowledge; but because of many hidden defects in men and women's bodies, they have a more civil way; for they have near every town a couple of pools (which they call Adam and Eve's pools), where it is permitted to one of the friends of the man, and another of the friends of the woman, to see them severally bathe naked.»

And as we were thus in conference, there came one that seemed to be a messenger, in a rich huke, that spake with the Jew; whereupon he turned to me and said, "You will pardon me, for I am commanded away in haste." The next morning he came to me again, joyful as it seemed and said, "There is word come to the governor of the city, that one of the fathers of Salomon's House will be here this day seven-night; we have seen none of them this dozen years. His coming is in state; but the cause of his coming is secret. I will provide you and your fellows of a good standing to see his entry." I thanked him, and told him I was most glad of the news. The day being come he made his entry. He was a man of middle stature and age, comely of person, and had an aspect as if he pitied men. He was clothed in a robe of fine black cloth with wide sleeves, and a cape; his under garment was of excellent white linen down to the foot, girt with a girdle of the same; and a sindon or tippet of the same about his neck. He had gloves that were curious, and set with stone; and shoes of peach-colored velvet. His neck was bare to the shoulders. His hat was like a helmet, or Spanish montero; and his locks curled below it decently; they were of color brown. His beard was cut round and of the same color with his hair, somewhat lighter. He was carried in a rich chariot, without wheels, litter-wise, with two horses at either end, richly trapped in blue velvet embroidered; and two footmen on each side in the like attire. The chariot was all of cedar, gilt, and adorned with crystal; save that the fore-end had panels of sapphires, set in borders of gold, and the hinder-end the like of emeralds of the Peru color. There was also a sun of gold, radiant upon the top, in the midst; and on the top before a small cherub of gold, with wings displayed. The chariot was covered with cloth of gold tissued upon blue. He had before him fifty attendants, young men all, in white satin loose coats up to the mid-leg, and stockings of white silk; and shoes of blue velvet; and hats of blue velvet, with fine plumes of divers colors, set round like hatbands. Next before the chariot went two men, bare-headed, in linen garments down to the foot, girt, and shoes of blue

velvet, who carried the one a crosier, the other a pastoral staff like a sheephook; neither of them of metal,
but the crosier of balm-wood, the pastoral staff of cedar.
Horsemen he had none, neither before nor behind his
chariot; as it seemeth, to avoid all tumult and trouble.
Behind his chariot went all the officers and principals of
the companies of the city. He sat alone, upon cushions,
of a kind of excellent plush, blue; and under his foot
curious carpets of silk of divers colors, like the Persian,
but far finer. He held up his bare hand, as he went, as
blessing the people, but in silence. The street was won-
derfully well kept; so that there was never any army
had their men stand in better battle-array than the people stood. The windows likewise were not crowded, but
everyone stood in them, as if they had been placed.
When the show was passed, the Jew said to me, "I shall
not be able to attend you as I would, in regard of some
charge the city hath laid upon me for the entertaining of
this great person." Three days after the Jew came to
me again, and said, "Ye are happy men; for the father
of Salomon's House taketh knowledge of your being here,
and commanded me to tell you, that he will admit all
your company to his presence, and have private conference with one of you, that ye shall choose; and for this
hath appointed the next day after to-morrow. And because he meaneth to give you his blessing, he hath appointed it in the forenoon." We came at our day and
hour, and I was chosen by my fellows for the private
access. We found him in a fair chamber, richly hanged,
and carpeted under foot, without any degrees to the
state; he was set upon a low throne richly adorned, and
a rich cloth of state over his head of blue satin embroidered. He was alone, save that he had two pages
of honor, on either hand one, finely attired in white.
His under garments were the like that we saw him wear
in the chariot; but instead of his gown, he had on him
a mantle with a cape, of the same fine black, fastened
about him. When we came in, as we were taught, we
bowed low at our first entrance; and when we were
come near his chair, he stood up, holding forth his hand
ungloved, and in posture of blessing; and we every one

of us stooped down, and kissed the end of his tippet. That done, the rest departed, and I remained. Then he warned the pages forth of the room, and caused me to sit down beside him, and spake to me thus in the Spanish tongue:—

"God bless thee, my son; I will give thee the greatest jewel I have. For I will impart unto thee, for the love of God and men, a relation of the true state of Salomon's House. Son, to make you know the true state of Salomon's House, I will keep this order. First, I will set forth unto you the end of our foundation. Secondly, the preparations and instruments we have for our works. Thirdly, the several employments and functions whereto our fellows are assigned. And fourthly, the ordinances and rites which we observe.

"The end of our foundation is the knowledge of causes, and secret motions of things; and the enlarging of the bounds of human empire, to the effecting of all things possible.

"The preparations and instruments are these. We have large and deep caves of several depths; the deepest are sunk 600 fathoms; and some of them are digged and made under great hills and mountains; so that if you reckon together the depth of the hill, and the depth of the cave, they are, some of them, above three miles deep. For we find that the depth of an hill, and the depth of a cave from the flat, is the same thing; both remote alike from the sun and heaven's beams, and from the open air. These caves we call the lower region. And we use them for all coagulations, indurations, refrigerations, and conservations of bodies. We use them likewise for the imitation of natural mines and the producing also of new artificial metals, by compositions and materials which we use and lay there for many years. We use them also sometimes (which may seem strange) for curing of some diseases, and for prolongation of life, in some hermits that choose to live there, well accommodated of all things necessary, and indeed live very long; by whom also we learn many things.

"We have burials in several earths, where we put divers cements, as the Chinese do their porcelain. But

we have them in greater variety, and some of them more
fine. We also have great variety of composts and soils,
for the making of the earth fruitful.

" We have high towers, the highest about half a mile
in height, and some of them likewise set upon high
mountains, so that the vantage of the hill with the
tower, is in the highest of them three miles at least.
And these places we call the upper region, account the
air between the high places and the low, as a middle
region. We use these towers, according to their several
heights and situations, for insulation, refrigeration, con-
servation, and for the view of divers meteors — as winds,
rain, snow, hail; and some of the fiery meteors also.
And upon them, in some places, are dwellings of hermits,
whom we visit sometimes, and instruct what to observe.

" We have great lakes, both salt and fresh, whereof we
have use for the fish and fowl. We use them also for
burials of some natural bodies, for we find a difference
in things buried in earth, or in air below the earth, and
things buried in water. We have also pools, of which
some do strain fresh water out of salt, and others by
art do turn fresh water into salt. We have also some
rocks in the midst of the sea, and some bays upon the
shore for some works, wherein is required the air and
vapor of the sea. We have likewise violent streams
and cataracts, which serve us for many motions; and
likewise engines for multiplying and enforcing of winds
to set also on divers motions.

" We have also a number of artificial wells and fountains, made in imitation of the natural sources and baths,
as tincted upon vitriol, sulphur, steel, brass, lead, niter,
and other minerals; and again, we have little wells for
infusions of many things; where the waters take the
virtue quicker and better than in vessels or basins. And
among them we have a water, which we call water of
Paradise, being by that we do it made very sovereign
for health and prolongation of life.

" We have also great and spacious houses, where we
imitate and demonstrate meteors — as snow, hail, rain,
some artificial rains of bodies, and not of water, thun-

ders, lightnings; also generations of bodies in air — as frogs flies, and divers others.

" We have also certain chambers, which we call chambers of health, where we qualify the air as we think good and proper for the cure of divers diseases, and preservation of health.

" We have also fair and large baths, of several mixtures, for the cure of diseases, and the restoring of man's body from arefaction; and others for the confirming of it in strength of sinews, vital parts, and the very juice and substance of the body.

" We have also large and various orchards and gardens, wherein we do not so much respect beauty as variety of ground and soil, proper for divers trees and herbs, and some very spacious, where trees and berries are set, whereof we make divers kinds of drinks, besides the vineyards. In these we practice likewise all conclusions of grafting, and inoculating, as well of wild trees as fruit trees, which produceth many effects. And we make by art, in the same orchards and gardens, trees and flowers, to come earlier or later than their seasons, and to come up and bear more speedily than by their natural course they do. We make them also by art greater much than their nature; and their fruit greater and sweeter, and of different taste, smell, color, and figure, from their nature. And many of them we so order, as that they become of medicinal use.

" We have also means to make divers plants rise by mixtures of earths without seeds, and likewise to make divers new plants, differing from the vulgar, and to make one tree or plant turn into another.

" We have also parks, and inclosures of all sorts, of beasts and birds; which we use not only for view or rareness, but likewise for dissections and trials, that thereby may take light what may be wrought upon the body of man. Wherein we find many strange effects: as continuing life in them, though divers parts, which you account vital, be perished and taken forth; resuscitating of some that seem dead in appearance, and the like. We try also all poisons, and other medicines upon them, as well of chirurgery as physic. By art likewise we make them greater or smaller than their kind is, and contrariwise dwarf them and stay their growth; we make them more fruitful and bearing than their kind is, and contrariwise barren and not generative. Also we make them differ in color, shape, activity, many ways. We find means to make commixtures and copulations of divers kinds, which have produced many new kinds, and them not barren, as the general opinion is. We make a number of kinds of serpents, worms, flies, fishes of putrefaction, whereof some are advanced (in effect) to be perfect creatures, like beasts or birds, and have sexes, and do propagate. Neither do we this by chance, but we know beforehand of what matter and commixture, what kind of those creatures will arise.

" We have also particular pools where we make trials upon fishes, as we have said before of beasts and birds.

" We have also places for breed and generation of those kinds of worms and flies which are of special use; such as are with you your silkworms and bees.

" I will not hold you long with recounting of our brewhouses, bake-houses, and kitchens, where are made divers drinks, breads, and meats, rare and of special effects. Wines we have of grapes, and drinks of other juice, of fruits, of grains, and of roots, and of mixtures with honey, sugar, manna, and fruits dried and decocted; also of the tears or wounding of trees, and of the pulp of canes. And these drinks are of several ages, some to the age or last of forty years. We have drinks also brewed with several herbs, and roots, and spices; yea, with several fleshes, and white meats; whereof some of the drinks are such as they are in effect meat and drink both, so that divers, especially in age, do desire to live with them with little or no meat or bread. And above all we strive to have drinks of extreme thin parts, to insinuate into the body, and yet without all biting, sharpness, or fretting; insomuch as some of them put upon the back of your hand, will with a little stay pass through to the palm, and yet taste mild to the mouth. We have also waters, which we ripen in that fashion, as they become nourishing, so that they are indeed excellent drinks, and many will use no other. Bread we have of several grains,

roots, and kernels; yea, and some of flesh, and fish, dried,
with divers kinds of leavings and seasonings; so that
some do extremely move appetites, some do nourish so,
as divers do live of them, without any other meat, who
live very long. So for meats, we have some of them so
beaten and made tender, and mortified, yet without all cor-
rupting, as a weak heat of the stomach will turn them
into good chilus, as well as a strong heat would meat
otherwise prepared. We have some meats also and bread,
and drinks, which taken by men, enable them to fast
long after; and some other, that used make the very
flesh of men's bodies sensibly more hard and tough, and
their strength far greater than otherwise it would be.

" We have dispensatories or shops of medicines; wherein
you may easily think, if we have such variety of plants,
and living creatures, more than you have in Europe (for
we know what you have), the simples, drugs, and in-
gredients of medicines, must likewise be in so much the
greater variety. We have them likewise of divers ages,
and long fermentations. And for their preparations, we
have not only all manner of exquisite distillations, and
separations, and especially by gentle heats, and percol-
ations through divers strainers, yea, and substances; but
also exact forms of composition, whereby they incorpo-
rate almost as they were natural simples.

" We have also divers mechanical arts, which you have
not; and stuffs made by them, as papers, linen, silks,
tissues, dainty works of feathers of wonderful luster, excellent dyes, and many others, and shops likewise as well
for such as are not brought into vulgar use among us,
as for those that are. For you must know, that of the
things before recited, many of them are grown into use
throughout the kingdom, but yet, if they did flow from
our invention, we have of them also for patterns and
principles.

" We have also furnaces of great diversities, and that
keep great diversity of heats; fierce and quick, strong
and constant, soft and mild, blown, quiet, dry, moist,
and the like. But above all we have heats, in imitation
of the sun's and heavenly bodies' heats, that pass divers
inequalities, and as it were orbs, progresses, and returns

whereby we produce admirable effects. Besides, we have heats of dungs, and of bellies and maws of living creatures and of their bloods and bodies, and of hays and herbs laid up moist, of lime unquenched, and such like. Instruments also which generate heat only by motion. And further, places for strong insulations; and again, places under the earth, which by nature or art yield heat. These divers heats we use, as the nature of the operation which we intend requireth.

" We have also perspective-houses, where we make demonstrations of all lights and radiations, and of all colors; and out of things uncolored and transparent, we can represent unto you all several colors, not in rainbows, as it is in gems and prisms, but of themselves single. We represent also all multiplications of light, which we carry to great distance, and make so sharp, as to discern small points and lines. Also all colorations of light: all delusions and deceits of the sight, in figures, magnitudes, motions, colors; all demonstrations of shadows. We find also divers means, yet unknown to you, of producing of light, originally from divers bodies. We procure means of seeing objects afar off, as in the heaven and remote places; and represent things near as afar off, and things afar off as near; making feigned distances. We have also helps for the sight far above spectacles and glasses in use; we have also glasses and means to see small and minute bodies, perfectly and distinctly; as the shapes and colors of small flies and worms, grains, and flaws in gems which cannot otherwise be seen, observations in urine and blood not otherwise to be seen. We make artificial rainbows, halos, and circles about light. We represent also all manner of reflections, refractions, and multiplications of visual beams of objects.

" We have also precious stones, of all kinds, many of them of great beauty and to you unknown; crystals likewise, and glasses of divers kind; and among them some of metals vitrificated, and other materials, besides those of which you make glass. Also a number of fossils, and imperfect minerals, which you have not. Likewise loadstones of prodigious virtue: and other rare stones, both natural and artificial.

"We have also sound-houses, where we practice and demonstrate all sounds and their generation. We have harmony which you have not, of quarter sounds and lesser slides of sounds. Divers instruments of music likewise to you unknown, some sweeter than any you have; with bells and rings that are dainty and sweet. We represent small sounds as great and deep, likewise great sounds, extenuate and sharp; we make divers tremblings and warblings of sounds, which in their original are entire. We represent and imitate all articulate sounds and letters, and the voices and notes of beasts and birds. We have certain helps, which set to the ear do further the hearing greatly; we have also divers strange and artificial echoes, reflecting the voice many times, and as it were tossing it; and some that give back the voice louder than it came, some shriller and some deeper; yea, some rendering the voice, differing in the letters or articulate sound from that they receive. We have all means to convey sounds in trunks and pipes, in strange lines and distances.

"We have also perfume-houses, wherewith we join also practices of taste. We multiply smells which may seem strange: we imitate smells, making all smells to breathe out of other mixtures than those that give them. We make divers imitations of taste likewise, so that they will deceive any man's taste. And in this house we contain also a confiture-house, where we make all sweetmeats, dry and moist, and divers pleasant wines, milks, broths, and salads, far in greater variety than you have.

" We have also engine-houses, where are prepared engines and instruments for all sorts of motions. There we imitate and practice to make swifter motions than any you have, either out of your muskets or any engine that you have; and to make them and multiply them more easily and with small force, by wheels and other means, and to make them stronger and more violent than yours are, exceeding your greatest cannons and basilisks. We represent also ordnance and instruments of war and engines of all kinds; and likewise new mixtures and compositions of gunpowder, wildfires burning in water and unquenchable, also fireworks of all variety, both for pleasure and use. We imitate also flights of birds; we have some degrees of flying in the air. We have ships and boats for going under water and brooking of seas, also swimming-girdles and supporters. We have divers curious clocks and other like motions of return, and some perpetual motions. We imitate also motions of living creatures by images of men, beasts, birds, fishes, and serpents; we have also a great number of other various motions, strange for equality, fineness and subtilty.

" We have also a mathematical-house, where are represented all instruments, as well of geometry as astronomy, exquisitely made.

" We have also houses of deceits of the senses, where we represent all manner of feats of juggling, false apparitions, impostures and illusions, and their fallacies. And surely you will easily believe that we, that have so many things truly natural which induce admiration, could in a world of particulars deceive the senses if we would disguise those things, and labor to make them more miraculous. But we do hate all impostures, and lies, insomuch as we have severely forbidden it to all our fellows, under pain of ignominy and fines, that they do not show any natural work or thing adorned or swelling, but only pure as it is, and without all affectation of strangeness.

" These are, my son, the riches of Salomon's House.

" For the several employments and offices of our fellows, we have twelve that sail into foreign countries under the names of other nations (for our own we conceal), who bring us the books and abstracts, and patterns of experiments of all other parts. These we call merchants of light.

" We have three that collect the experiments which are in all books. These we call deprepators.

" We have three that collect the experiments of all mechanical arts, and also of liberal sciences, and also of practices which are not brought into arts. These we call mystery-men.

" We have three that try new experiments.

" Such as themselves think good. These we call pioneers or miners.

" We have three that draw the experiments of the former four into titles and tables, to give the better light for the drawing of observations and axioms out of them. These we call compilers. We have three that bend themselves, looking into the experiments of their fellows, and cast about how to draw out of them things of use and practice for man's life and knowledge, as well for works as for plain demonstration of causes, means of natural divinations, and the easy and clear discovery of the virtues and parts of bodies. These we call dowrymen or benefactors.

"Then after divers meetings and consults of our whole number, to consider of the former labors and collections, we have three that take care out of them to direct new experiments, of a higher light, more penetrating into Nature than the former. These we call lamps.

"We have three others that do execute the experiments so directed, and report them. These we call inoculators.

"Lastly, we have three that raise the former discoveries by experiments into greater observations, axioms, and aphorisms. These we call interpreters of Nature.

"We have also, as you must think, novices and apprentices, that the succession of the former employed men do not fail; besides a great number of servants and attendants, men and women. And this we do also: we have consultations, which of the inventions and experiences which we have discovered shall be published, and which not: and take all an oath of secrecy for the concealing of those which we think fit to keep secret: though some of those we do reveal sometime to the state, and some not.

"For our ordinances and rites, we have two very long and fair galleries: in one of these we place patterns and samples of all manner of the more rare and excellent inventions: in the other we place the statues of all principal inventors. There we have the statue of your Columbus, that discovered the West Indies: also the inventor of ships: your Monk that was the inventor of ordnance and of gunpowder: the inventor of music: the inventor of letters: the inventor of printing: the inventor of observations of astronomy: the inventor of works in metal: the inventor of glass: the inventor of silk of the worm: the inventor of wine: the inventor of corn and bread: the inventor of sugars; and all these by more certain tradition than you have. Then we have divers inventors of our own, of excellent works; which since you have not seen, it were too long to make descriptions of them; and besides, in the right understanding of those descriptions you might easily err. For upon every invention of value we erect a statue to the inventor, and give him a liberal and honorable reward. These statues are some of brass, some of marble and touchstone, some of cedar and other special woods gilt and adorned; some of iron, some of silver, some of gold.

"We have certain hymns and services, which we say daily, of laud and thanks to God for his marvelous works. And forms of prayers, imploring his aid and blessing for the illumination of our labors; and turning them into good and holy uses.

"Lastly, we have circuits or visits, of divers principal cities of the kingdom; where as it cometh to pass we do publish such new profitable inventions as we think good. And we do also declare natural divinations of diseases, plagues, swarms of hurtful creatures, scarcity, tempest, earthquakes, great inundations, comets, temperature of the year and divers other things; and we give counsel thereupon, what the people shall do for the prevention and remedy of them."

And when he had said this, he stood up; and I, as I had been taught, knelt down; and he laid his right hand upon my head, and said, "God bless thee, my son, and God bless this relation which I have made. I give thee leave to publish it, for the good of other nations; for we here are in God's bosom, a land unknown." And so he left me; having assigned a value of about two thousand ducats for a bounty to me and my fellows. For they give great largesses, where they come, upon all occasions.

THE REST WAS NOT PERFECTED.

CAMPANELLA'S

CITY OF THE SUN.

THE CITY OF THE SUN.

[A Poetical Dialogue between a Grandmaster of the Knights Hospitallers and a Genoese Sea Captain, his Guest.]

G. M.—Prithee, now, tell me what happened to you during that voyage?

Capt.—I have already told you how I wandered over the whole earth. In the course of my journeying I came to Taprobane, and was compelled to go ashore at a place, where through fear of the inhabitants I remained in a wood. When I stepped out of this I found myself on a large plain immediately under the equator.

G. M.—And what befell you here?

Capt.—I came upon a large crowd of men and armed women, many of whom did not understand our language, and they conducted me forthwith to the City of the Sun.

G. M.—Tell me after what plan this city is built and how it is governed?

Capt.—The greater part of the city is built upon a high hill, which rises from an extensive plain, but several of its circles extend for some distance beyond the base of the hill, which is of such a size that the diameter of the city is upward of two miles, so that its circumference becomes about seven. On account of the humped shape of the mountain, however, the diameter of the city is really more than if it were built on a plain.

It is divided into seven rings or huge circles named from the seven planets, and the way from one to the other of these is by four streets and through four gates, that look toward the four points of the compass. Furthermore, it is so built that if the first circle were stormed, it would of necessity entail a double amount of energy to storm the second; still more to storm the third; and in each succeeding case the strength and energy would have to be doubled; so that he who wishes to capture that city must, as it were, storm it seven times. For my own part, however, I think that not even the first wall could be occupied, so thick are the earthworks and so well fortified is it with breastworks, towers, guns and ditches.

When I had been taken through the northern gate (which is shut with an iron door so wrought that it can be raised and let down, and locked in easily and strongly, its projections running into the grooves of the thick posts by a marvelous device), I saw a level space seventy paces * wide between the first and second walls. From hence can be seen large palaces all joined to the wall of the second circuit, in such a manner as to appear all one palace. Arches run on a level with the middle height of the palaces, and are continued round the whole ring. There are galleries for promenading upon these arches, which are supported from beneath by thick and well-shaped columns, enclosing arcades like peristyles, or cloisters of an abbey.

But the palaces have no entrances from below except on the inner or concave partition, from which one enters directly to the lower parts of the building. The higher parts, however, are reached by flights of marble steps, which lead to galleries for promenading on the inside similar to those on the outside. From these one enters the higher rooms, which are very beautiful, and have windows on the concave and convex partitions. These rooms are divided from one another by richly decorated walls. The convex or outer wall of the ring is about eight spans thick; the concave three; the intermediate walls are one, or perhaps one and a half. Leaving this circle one gets to the second plain, which is nearly three paces narrower than the first. Then the first wall of the second ring is seen adorned above and below with similar galleries for walking, and there is on the inside of it another interior wall inclosing palaces. It has also similar peristyles supported by columns in the lower part, but above are excellent pictures, round the ways into the upper houses. And so on afterward through similar spaces and double walls, enclosing palaces, and

* A pace was $1\frac{9}{25}$ yards, 1,000 paces making a mile.

adorned with galleries for walking, extending along their outer side and supported by columns, till the last circuit is reached the way being still over a level plain.

But when the two gates, that is to say, those of the outmost and the inmost walls have been passed, one mounts by means of steps so formed that an ascent is scarcely discernible, since it proceeds in a slanting direction, and the steps succeed one another at almost imperceptible heights. On the top of the hill is a rather spacious plain, and in the midst of this there rises a temple built with wondrous art.

G. M.—Tell on, I pray you! Tell on! I am dying to hear more.

Capt.—The temple is built in the form of a circle; it is not girt with walls, but stands upon thick columns, beautifully grouped. A very large dome, built with great care in the center or pole, contains another small vault as it were rising out of it, and in this a spiracle, which is right over the altar. There is but one altar in the middle of the temple, and this is hedged round by columns. The temple itself is on a space of more than three hundred and fifty paces. Without it, arches measuring about eight paces extend from the heads of the columns outwards, whence other columns rise about three paces from the thick, strong and erect wall. Between these and the former columns there are galleries for walking, with beautiful pavements, and in the recess of the wall, which is adorned with numerous large doors, there are immovable seats, placed as it were between the inside columns, supporting the temple. Portable chairs are not wanting, many and well adorned. Nothing is seen over the altar but a large globe, upon which the heavenly bodies are painted, and another globe upon which there is a representation of the earth. Furthermore, in the vault of the dome there can be discerned representations of all the stars of heaven from the first to the sixth magnitude, with their proper names and power—to influence terrestrial things marked in three little verses for each. There are the poles and greater and lesser circles according to the right latitude of the place, but these are not perfect because there is no wall below. They seem, too, to be made in their relation to the globes on the altar. The pavement of the temple is bright with precious stones. Its seven golden lamps hang always burning, and these bear the names of the seven planets.

At the top of the building several small and beautiful cells surround the small dome, and behind the level space above the bands or arches of the exterior and interior columns there are many cells, both small and large, where the priests and religious officers dwell to the number of forty-nine.

A revolving flag projects from the smaller dome, and this shows in what quarter the wind is. The flag is marked with figures up to thirty-six, and the priests know what sort of year the different kinds of winds bring and what will be the changes of weather on land and sea. Furthermore, under the flag a book is always kept written with letters of gold.

G. M.—I pray you, worthy hero, explain to me their whole system of government; for I am anxious to hear it.

Capt.—The great ruler among them is a priest whom they call by the name Hoh, though we should call him Metaphysic. He is head over all, in temporal and spiritual matters, and all business and lawsuits are settled by him, as the supreme authority. Three princes of equal power — viz, Pon, Sin and Mor — assist him, and these in our tongue we should call Power, Wisdom and Love. To Power belongs the care of all matters relating to war and peace. He attends to the military arts, and, next to Hoh, he is ruler in every affair of a warlike nature. He governs the military magistrates and the soldiers, and has the management of the munitions, the fortifications, the storming of places, the implements of war, the armories, the smiths and workmen connected with matters of this sort.

But Wisdom is the ruler of the liberal arts, of mechanics, of all sciences with their magistrates and doctors, and of the discipline of the schools. As many doctors as there are, are under his control. There is one doctor who is called Astrologus; a second, Cosmographus; a third, Arithmeticus; a fourth, Geometra; a fifth, Historiographus; a sixth, Poeta; a seventh, Logicus; an eighth, Rhetor; a ninth, Grammaticus; a tenth, Medicus;

an eleventh, Physiologus; a twelfth, Politicus; a thirteenth, Moralis. They have but one book, which they call Wisdom, and in it all the sciences are written with conciseness and marvelous fluency of expression. This they read to the people after the custom of the Pythagoreans. It is Wisdom who causes the exterior and interior, the higher and lower walls of the city to be adorned with the finest pictures, and to have all the sciences painted upon them in an admirable manner. On the walls of the temple and on the dome, which is let down when the priest gives an address, lest the sounds of his voice, being scattered, should fly away from his audience, there are pictures of stars in their different magnitudes, with the powers and motions of each, expressed separately in three little verses.

On the interior wall of the first circuit all the mathematical figures are conspicuously painted — figures more in number than Archimedes or Euclid discovered, marked symmetrically, and with the explanation of them neatly written and contained each in a little verse. There are definitions and propositions, etc., etc. On the exterior convex wall is first an immense drawing of the whole earth, given at one view. Following upon this, there are tablets setting forth for every separate country the customs both public and private, the laws, the origins and the power of the inhabitants; and the alphabets the different people use can be seen above that of the City of the Sun.

On the inside of the second circuit, that is to say of the second ring of buildings, paintings of all kinds of precious and common stones, of minerals and metals are seen; and a little piece of the metal itself is also there with an apposite explanation in two small verses for each metal or stone. On the outside are marked all the seas, rivers, lakes, and streams which are on the face of the earth; as are also the wines and the oils and the different liquids, with the sources from which the last are extracted, their qualities and strength. There are also vessels built into the wall above the arches, and these are full of liquids from one to three hundred years old, which cure all diseases. Hail and snow, storms and thunder, and whatever else takes place in the air, are represented with suitable figures and little verses. The inhabitants even have the art of representing in stone all the phenomena of the air, such as the wind, rain, thunder, the rainbow, etc.

On the interior of the third circuit all the different families of trees and herbs are depicted, and there is a live specimen of each plant in earthenware vessels placed upon the outer partition of the arches. With the specimens there are explanations as to where they were first found, what are their powers and natures, and resemblances to celestial things and to metals: to parts of the human body and to things in the sea, and also as to their uses in medicine, etc. On the exterior wall are all the races of fish, found in rivers, lakes and seas, and their habits and values, and ways of breeding, training and living, the purposes for which they exist in the world, and their uses to man. Further, their resemblances to celestial and terrestrial things, produced both by nature and art, are so given that I was astonished when I saw a fish which was like a bishop, one like a chain, another like a garment, a fourth like a nail, a fifth like a star, and others like images of those things existing among us, the relation in each case being completely manifest. There are sea urchins to be seen, and the purple shell-fish and mussels; and whatever the watery world possesses worthy of being known is there fully shown in marvelous characters of painting and drawing.

On the fourth interior wall all the different kinds of birds are painted, with their natures, sizes, customs, colors, manner of living, etc.; and the only real phœnix is possessed by the inhabitants of this city. On the exterior are shown all the races of creeping animals, serpents, dragons and worms; the insects, the flies, gnats, beetles, etc., in their different states, strength, venoms and uses, and a great deal more than you or I can think of.

On the fifth interior they have all the larger animals of the earth, as many in number as would astonish you. We indeed know not the thousandth part of them, for on the exterior wall also a great many of immense size are also portrayed. To be sure, of horses alone, how great a number of breeds there is and how beautiful are the forms there cleverly displayed

On the sixth interior are painted all the mechanical arts, with the several instruments for each and their manner of use among different nations. Alongside the dignity of such is placed, and their several inventors are named. But on the exterior all the inventors in science, in warfare, and in law are represented. There I saw Moses, Osiris, Jupiter, Mercury, Lycurgus, Pompilius, Pythagoras, Zamolxis, Solon, Charondas, Phoroneus, with very many others. They even have Mahomet, whom nevertheless they hate as a false and sordid legislator. In the most dignified position I saw a representation of Jesus Christ and of the twelve Apostles, whom they consider very worthy and hold to be great. Of the representations of men, I perceived Cæsar, Alexander, Pyrrhus and Hannibal in the highest place; and other very renowned heroes in peace and war, especially Roman heroes, were painted in lower positions, under the galleries. And when I asked with astonishment whence they had obtained our history, they told me that among them there was a knowledge of all languages, and that by perseverance they continually send explorers and ambassadors over the whole earth, who learn thoroughly the customs, forces, rule, and histories of the nations, bad and good alike. These they apply all to their own republic, and with this they are well pleased. I learned that cannon and typography were invented by the Chinese before we knew of them. There are magistrates, who announce the meaning of the pictures, and boys are accustomed to learn all the sciences, without toil and as if for pleasure; but in the way of history only until they are ten years old.

Love is foremost in attending to the charge of the race. He sees that men and women are so joined together, that they bring forth the best offspring. Indeed, they laugh at us who exhibit a studious care for our breed of horses and dogs, but neglect the breeding of human beings. Thus the education of the children is under his rule. So also is the medicine that is sold, the sowing and collecting of fruits of the earth and of trees.

agriculture, pasturage, the preparations for the months, the cooking arrangements, and whatever has any reference to food, clothing, and the intercourse of the sexes. Love himself is ruler, but there are many male and female magistrates dedicated to these arts.

Metaphysic then with these three rulers manage all the above-named matters, and even by himself alone nothing is done; all business is discharged by the four together, but in whatever Metaphysic inclines to the rest are sure to agree.

G. M.— Tell me, please, of the magistrates, their services and duties, of the education and mode of living, whether the government is a monarchy, a republic, or an aristocracy.

Capt.— This race of men came there from India, flying from the sword of the Magi, a race of plunderers and tyrants who laid waste their country, and they determined to lead a philosophic life in fellowship with one another. Although the community of wives is not instituted among the other inhabitants of their province, among them it is in use after this manner. All things are common with them, and their dispensation is by the authority of the magistrates. Arts and honors and pleasures are common, and are held in such a manner that no one can appropriate anything to himself.

They say that all private property is acquired and improved for the reason that each one of us by himself has his own home and wife and children. From this self-love springs. For when we raise a son to riches and dignities, and leave an heir to much wealth, we become either ready to grasp at the property of the state, if in any case fear should be removed from the power which belongs to riches and rank; or avaricious, crafty, and hypocritical, if anyone is of slender purse, little strength, and mean ancestry. But when we have taken away self-love, there remains only love for the state.

G. M.— Under such circumstances no one will be willing to labor, while he expects others to work, on the fruit of whose labors he can live, as Aristotle argues against Plato.

Capt.— I do not know how to deal with that argument, but I declare to you that they burn with so great a love for their fatherland, as I could scarcely have believed possible; and indeed with much more than the histories tell us belonged to the Romans, who fell willingly for their country, inasmuch as they have to a greater extent surrendered their private property. I think truly that the friars and monks and clergy of our country, if they were not weakened by love for their kindred and friends, or by the ambition to rise to higher dignities, would be less fond of property, and more imbued with a spirit of charity toward all, as it was in the time of the Apostles, and is now in a great many cases.

G. M. — St. Augustine may say that, but I say that among this race of men, friendship is worth nothing; since they have not the chance of conferring mutual benefits on one another.

Capt. — Nay, indeed. For it is worth the trouble to see that no one can receive gifts from another. Whatever is necessary they have, they receive it from the community, and the magistrate takes care that no one receives more than he deserves. Yet nothing necessary is denied to anyone. Friendship is recognized among them in war, in infirmity, in the art contests, by which means they aid one another mutually by teaching. Sometimes they improve themselves mutually with praises, with conversation, with actions, and out of the things they need. All those of the same age call one another brothers. They call all over twenty-two years of age, fathers; those who are less than twenty-two are named sons. Moreover, the magistrates govern well, so that no one in the fraternity can do injury to another.

G. M. — And how ?

Capt. — As many names of virtues as there are among us, so many magistrates there are among them. There is a magistrate who is named Magnanimity, another Fortitude, a third Chastity, a fourth Liberality, a fifth Criminal and Civil Justice, a sixth Comfort, a seventh Truth, an eighth Kindness, a tenth Gratitude, an eleventh Cheerfulness, a twelfth Exercise, a thirteenth Sobriety, etc. They are elected to duties of that kind, each one to that duty for excellence in which he is known from boyhood to be most suitable. Wherefore among them neither robbery nor clever murders, nor lewdness, incest, adultery, or other crimes of which we accuse one another, can be found. They accuse themselves of ingratitude and malignity when anyone denies a lawful satisfaction to another, of indolence, of sadness, of anger, of scurrility, of slander, and of lying, which curseful thing they thoroughly hate. Accused persons undergoing punishment are deprived of the common table, and other honors, until the judge thinks that they agree with their correction.

G. M.— Tell me the manner in which the magistrates are chosen.

Capt.— You would not rightly understand this, unless you first learned their manner of living. That you may know then, men and women wear the same kind of garment, suited for war. The women wear the toga below the knee, but the men above. And both sexes are instructed in all the arts together. When this has been done as a start, and before their third year, the boys learn the language and the alphabet on the walls by walking round them. They have four leaders, and four elders, the first to direct them, the second to teach them and these are men approved beyond all others. After some time they exercise themselves, with gymnastics, running, quoits, and other games, by means of which all their muscles are strengthened alike. Their feet are always bare, and so are their heads as far as the seventh ring. Afterward they lead them to the offices of the trades, such as shoemaking, cooking, metalworking, carpentry, painting, etc. In order to find out the bent of the genius of each one, after their seventh year, when they have already gone through the mathematics on the walls, they take them to the readings of all the sciences; there are four lectures at each reading, and in the course of four hours the four in their order explain everything.

For some take physical exercise or busy themselves with public services or functions, others apply themselves to reading. Leaving these studies all are devoted to the more abstruse subjects, to mathematics, to medicine, and to other sciences. There is continual debate

and studied argument among them, and after a time
they become magistrates of those sciences or mechanical
arts in which they are the most proficient; for every
one follows the opinion of his leader and judge, and
goes out to the plains to the works of the field, and for
the purpose of becoming acquainted with the pasturage
of the dumb animals. And they consider him the more
noble and renowned who has dedicated himself to the
study of the most arts and knows how to practice them
wisely. Wherefore they laugh at us in that we consider
our workmen ignoble, and hold those to be noble who
have mastered no pursuit; but live in ease, and are so
many slaves given over to their own pleasure and lasciviousness; and thus as it were from a school of vices
so many idle and wicked fellows go forth for the ruin
of the state.

The rest of the officials, however, are chosen by the
four chiefs, Hoh, Pon, Sin and Mor, and by the teachers of that art over which they are fit to preside. And
these teachers know well who is most suited for rule.
Certain men are proposed by the magistrates in council,
they themselves not seeking to become candidates, and
he opposes who knows anything against those brought
forward for election, or if not, speaks in favor of them.
But no one attains to the dignity of Hoh except him
who knows the histories of the nations, and their customs and sacrifices and laws, and their form of government, whether a republic or a monarchy. He must also
know the names of the lawgivers and the inventors in
science, and the laws and the history of the earth and
the heavenly bodies. They think it also necessary
that he should understand all the mechanical arts, the
physical sciences, astrology and mathematics. (Nearly
every two days they teach our mechanical art. They
are not allowed to overwork themselves, but frequent
practice and the paintings render learning easy to them.
Not too much care is given to the cultivation of languages, as they have a goodly number of interpreters
who are grammarians in the state.) But beyond everything else it is necessary that Hoh should understand
metaphysics and theology; that he should know thoroughly

the derivations, foundations and demonstrations of all the arts and sciences; the likeness and difference of things; necessity, fate, and the harmonies of the universe; power, wisdom, and the love of things and of God; the stages of life and its symbols; everything relating to the heavens, the earth and the sea; and the ideas of God, as much as mortal man can know of him. He must also be well read in the Prophets and in astrology. And thus they know long beforehand who will be Hoh. He is not chosen to so great a dignity unless he has attained his thirty-fifth year. And this office is perpetual, because it is not known who may be too wise for it or who too skilled in ruling.

G. M.—Who indeed can be so wise? If even anyone has a knowledge of the sciences it seems that he must be unskilled in ruling.

Capt.—This very question I asked them and they replied thus: "We, indeed, are more certain that such a very learned man has the knowledge of governing, than you who place ignorant persons in authority, and consider them suitable merely because they have sprung from rulers or have been chosen by a powerful faction. But our Hoh, a man really the most capable to rule, is for all that never cruel nor wicked, nor a tyrant, inasmuch as he possesses so much wisdom. This, moreover, is not unknown to you, that the same argument cannot apply among you, when you consider that man the most learned who knows most of grammar, or logic, or of Aristotle or any other author. For such knowledge as this of yours much servile labor and memory work is required, so that a man is rendered unskillful; since he has contemplated nothing but the words of books and has given his mind with useless result to the consideration of the dead signs of things. Hence he knows not in what way God rules the universe, nor the ways and customs of Nature and the nations. Wherefore he is not equal to our Hoh. For that one cannot know so many arts and sciences thoroughly, who is not esteemed for skilled ingenuity, very apt at all things, and therefore at ruling especially. This also is plain to us that he who knows only one science, does not really know either that or the others, and he who is suited for only one science and has gathered his knowledge from books, is unlearned and unskilled. But this is not the case with intellects prompt and expert in every branch of knowledge and suitable for the consideration of natural objects, as it is necessary that our HOH should be. Besides in our state the sciences are taught with a facility (as you have seen) by which more scholars are turned out by us in one year than by you in ten, or even fifteen. Make trial, I pray you, of these boys." In this matter I was struck with astonishment at their truthful discourse and at the trial of their boys, who did not understand my language well. Indeed it is necessary that three of them should be skilled in our tongue, three in Arabic, three in Polish, and three in each of the other languages, and no recreation is allowed them unless they become more learned. For that they go out to the plain for the sake of running about and hurling arrows and lances, and of firing harquebuses, and for the sake of hunting the wild animals and getting a knowledge of plants and stones, and agriculture and pasturage; sometimes the band of boys does one thing, sometimes another.

They do not consider it necessary that the three rulers assisting HOH should know other than the arts having reference to their rule, and so they have only a historical knowledge of the arts which are common to all. But their own they know well, to which certainly one is dedicated more than another. Thus POWER is the most learned in the equestrian art, in marshaling the army, in marking out of camps, in the manufacture of every kind of weapon and of warlike machines, in planning stratagems, and in every affair of a military nature. And for these reasons, they consider it necessary that these chiefs should have been philosophers, historians, politicians, and physicists. Concerning the other two triumvirs, understand remarks similar to those I have made about POWER.

G. M.— I really wish that you would recount all their public duties, and would distinguish between them, and also that you would tell clearly how they are all taught in common.

Capt.— They have dwellings in common and dormitories, and couches and other necessaries. But at the end of every six months they are separated by the masters. Some shall sleep in this ring, some in another; some in the first apartment, and some in the second; and these apartments are marked by means of the alphabet on the lintel. There are occupations, mechanical and theoretical, common to both men and women, with this difference, that the occupations which require more hard work, and walking a long distance, are practiced by men, such as plowing, sowing, gathering the fruits, working at the threshing-floor, and perchance at the vintage. But it is customary to choose women for milking the cows, and for making cheese. In like manner, they go to the gardens near to the outskirts of the city both for collecting the plants and for cultivating them. In fact, all sedentary and stationary pursuits are practiced by the women, such as weaving, spinning, sewing, cutting the hair, shaving, dispensing medicines, and making all kinds of garments. They are, however, excluded from working in wood and the manufacture of arms. If a woman is fit to paint, she is not prevented from doing so; nevertheless, music is given over to the women alone, because they please the more, and of a truth to boys also. But the women have not the practice of the drum and the horn.

And they prepare their feasts and arrange the tables in the following manner. It is the peculiar work of the boys and girls under twenty to wait at the tables. In every ring there are the suitable kitchens, barns, and stores of utensils for eating and drinking, and over every department an old man and an old woman preside. These two have at once the command of those who serve, and the power of chastising or causing to be chastised, those who are negligent or disobedient; and they also examine and mark each one, both male and female, who excels in his or her duties.

All the young people wait upon the older ones who have passed the age of forty, and in the evening when they go to sleep the master and mistress command that those should be sent to work in the morning, upon whom in succession the duty falls, one or two to separate apartments. The young people, however, wait upon one another, and that alas! with some unwillingness. They have first and second tables, and on both sides there are seats. On one side sit the women, on the other the men; and as in the refectories of the monks, there is no noise. While they are eating a young man reads a book from a platform, intoning distinctly and sonorously, and often the magistrates question them upon the more important parts of the reading. And truly it is pleasant to observe in what manner these young people, so beautiful and clothed in garments so suitable, attend to them, and to see at the same time so many friends, brothers, sons, fathers and mothers all in their turn living together with so much honesty, propriety and love. So each one is given a napkin, a plate, fish, and a dish of food. It is the duty of the medical officers to tell the cooks what repasts shall be prepared on each day, and what food for the old, what for the young, and what for the sick. The magistrates receive the full-grown and fatter portion, and they from their share always distribute something to the boys at the table who have shown themselves more studious in the morning at the lectures and debates concerning wisdom and arms. And this is held to be one of the most distinguished honors. For six days they ordain to sing with music at table. Only a few, however, sing; or there is one voice accompanying the lute and one for each other instrument. And when all alike in service join their hands, nothing is found to be wanting. The old men placed at the head of the cooking business and of the refectories of the servants praise the cleanliness of the streets, the houses, the vessels, the garments, the workshops and the warehouses.

They wear white undergarments to which adheres a covering, which is at once coat and legging, without wrinkles. The borders of the fastenings are furnished with globular buttons, extended round and caught up here and there by chains. The coverings of the legs descend to the shoes and are continued even to the heels. Then they cover the feet with large socks, or as it were half-buskins fastened by buckles, over which they wear a half-boot, and besides, as I have already said, they are clothed with a toga. And so aptly fitting are the garments, that when the toga is destroyed, the different parts of the whole body are straightway discerned, no part being concealed. They change their clothes for different ones four times in the year, that is when the sun enters respectively the constellations Aries, Cancer, Libra and Capricorn, and according to the circumstances and necessity as decided by the officer of health. The keepers of clothes for the different rings are wont to distribute them, and it is marvelous that they have at the same time as many garments as there is need for, some heavy and some slight, according to the weather. They all use white clothing, and this is washed in each month with lye or soap, as are also the workshops of the lower trades, the kitchens, the pantries, the barns, the storehouses, the armories, the refectories, and the baths. Moreover, the clothes are washed at the pillars of the peristyles, and the water is brought down by means of canals which are continued as sewers. In every street of the different rings there are suitable fountains, which send forth their water by means of canals, the water being drawn up from nearly the bottom of the mountain by the sole movement of a cleverly contrived handle. There is water in fountains and in cisterns, whither the rain water collected from the roofs of the houses is brought through pipes full of sand. They wash their bodies often, according as the doctor and master command. All the mechanical arts are practiced under the peristyles, but the speculative are carried on above in the walking galleries and ramparts where are the more splendid paintings, but the more sacred ones are taught in the temple. In the halls and wings of the rings there are solar timepieces and bells, and hands by which the hours and seasons are marked off.

G. M. — Tell me about their children.

Capt. — When their women have brought forth children, they suckle and rear them in temples set apart for all. They give milk for two years or more as the physician orders. After that time the weaned child is given into the charge of the mistresses, if it is a female, and to the masters, if it is a male. And then with other young children they are pleasantly instructed in the alphabet, and in the knowledge of the pictures, and in running, walking and wrestling; also in the historical drawings, and in languages; and they are adorned with a suitable garment of different colors. After their sixth year they are taught natural science, and then the mechanical sciences. The men who are weak in intellect are sent to farms, and when they have become more proficient some of them are received into the state. And those of the same age and born under the same constellation are especially like one another in strength and in appearance, and hence arises much lasting concord in the state, these men honoring one another with mutual love and help. Names are given to them by Metaphysicus, and that not by chance but designedly, and according to each one's peculiarity, as was the custom among the ancient Romans. Wherefore one is called Beautiful (*Pulcher*), another the Big-nosed (*Naso*), another the Fat-legged (*Cranipes*), another Crooked (*Torvus*), another Lean (*Macer*), and so on. But when they have become very skilled in their professions and done any great deed in war or in time of peace, a cognomen from art is given to them, such as Beautiful the great painter (*Pulcher, Pictor Magnus*), the golden one (*Aureus*), the excellent one (*Excellens*), or the strong (*Strenuus*); or from their deeds, such as Naso the Brave (*Nason Fortis*), or the cunning, or the great, or very great conqueror; or from the enemy any one has overcome, Africanus, Asiaticus, Etruscus; or if any one has overcome Manfred or Tortelius, he is called Macer Manfred or Tortelius, and so on. All these cognomens are added by the higher magistrates, and very often with a crown suitable to the deed or art, and with the flourish of music. For gold and silver is reckoned of little value among them except as material for their vessels and ornaments, which are common to all.

G. M.—Tell me, I pray you, is there no jealousy among them or disappointment to that one who has not been elected to a magistracy, or to any other dignity to which he aspires?

Capt.—Certainly not. For no one wants either necessaries or luxuries. Moreover, the race is managed for

the good of the commonwealth and not of private individuals, and the magistrates must be obeyed. They deny
what we hold — viz, that it is natural to man to recog-
nize his offspring and to educate them, and to use his
wife and house and children as his own. For they say
that children are bred for the preservation of the species
and not for individual pleasure, as St. Thomas also as-
serts. Therefore the breeding of children has reference
to the commonwealth and not to individuals, except in
so far as they are constituents of the commonwealth.
And since individuals for the most part bring forth children wrongly and educate them wrongly, they consider
that they remove destruction from the state, and, therefore, for this reason, with most sacred fear, they commit
the education of the children, who as it were are the ele-
ment of the republic, to the care of magistrates; for the
safety of the community is not that of a few. And thus
they distribute male and female breeders of the best natures according to philosophical rules. Plato thinks that
this distribution ought to be made by lot, lest some men
seeing that they are kept away from the beautiful women,
should rise up with anger and hatred against the magistrates; and he thinks further that those who do not deserve cohabitation with the more beautiful women, should
be deceived whilst the lots are being led out of the city
by the magistrates, so that at all times the women who
are suitable should fall to their lot, not those whom they
desire. This shrewdness, however, is not necessary among
the inhabitants of the City of the Sun. For with them
deformity is unknown. When the women are exercised
they get a clear complexion, and become strong of limb,
tall and agile, and with them beauty consists in tallness
and strength. Therefore, if any woman dyes her face,
so that it may become beautiful, or uses high-heeled
boots so that she may appear tall, or garments with
trains to cover her wooden shoes, she is condemned to
capital punishment. But if the women should even desire them, they have no facility for doing these things.
For who indeed would give them this facility? Further,
they assert that among us abuses of this kind arise from
the leisure and sloth of women. By these means they

lose their color and have pale complexions, and become feeble and small. For this reason they are without proper complexions, use high sandals, and become beautiful not from strength, but from slothful tenderness. And thus they ruin their own tempers and natures, and consequently those of their offspring. Furthermore, if at any time a man is taken captive with ardent love for a certain woman, the two are allowed to converse and joke together, and to give one another garlands of flowers or leaves, and to make verses. But if the race is endangered, by no means is further union between them permitted. Moreover, the love born of eager desire is not known among them; only that born of friendship.

Domestic affairs and partnerships are of little account, because, excepting the sign of honor, each one receives what he is in need of. To the heroes and heroines of the republic, it is customary to give the pleasing gifts of honor, beautiful wreaths, sweet food, or splendid clothes, while they are feasting. In the daytime all use white garments within the city, but at night or outside the city they use red garments either of wool or silk. They hate black as they do dung, and therefore they dislike the Japanese, who are fond of black. Pride they consider the most execrable vice, and one who acts proudly is chastised with the most ruthless correction. Wherefore no one thinks it lowering to wait at table or to work in the kitchen or fields. All work they call discipline, and thus they say that it is honorable to go on foot, to do any act of nature, to see with the eye, and to speak with the tongue; and when there is need, they distinguish philosophically between tears and spittle.

Every man who, when he is told off to work, does his duty, is considered very honorable. It is not the custom to keep slaves. For they are enough, and more than enough, for themselves. But with us, alas! it is not so. In Naples there exist seventy thousand souls, and out of these scarcely ten or fifteen thousand do any work, and they are always lean from overwork and are getting weaker every day. The rest become a prey to idleness, avarice, ill-health, lasciviousness, usury and other vices, and contaminate and corrupt very many families by holding them in servitude for their own use, by keeping them in poverty and slavishness, and by imparting to them their own vices. Therefore public slavery ruins them; useful works, in the field, in military service, and in arts, except those which are debasing, are not cultivated, the few who do practice them doing so with much aversion. But in the City of the Sun, while duty and work is distributed among all, it only falls to each one to work for about four hours every day. The remaining hours are spent in learning joyously, in debating, in reading, in reciting, in writing, in walking, in exercising the mind and body, and with play. They allow no game which is played while sitting, neither the single die nor dice, nor chess, nor others like these. But they play with the ball, with the sack, with the hoop, with wrestling, with hurling at the stake. They say, moreover, that grinding poverty renders men worthless, cunning, sulky, thievish, insidious, vagabonds, liars, false witnesses, etc.; and that wealth makes them insolent, proud, ignorant, traitors, assumers of what they know not, deceivers, boasters, wanting in affection, slanderers, etc. But with them all the rich and poor together make up the community. They are rich because they want nothing, poor because they possess nothing; and consequently they are not slaves to circumstances, but circumstances serve them. And on this point they strongly recommend the religion of the Christians, and especially the life of the Apostles.

G. M.— This seems excellent and sacred, but the community of women is a thing too difficult to attain. The holy Roman Clement says that wives ought to be common in accordance with the apostolic institution, and praises Plato and Socrates, who thus teach, but the Glossary interprets this community with regard to obedience. And Tertullian agrees with the Glossary, that the first Christians had everything in common except wives.

Capt.— These things I know little of. But this I saw among the inhabitants of the City of the Sun that they did not make this exception. And they defend themselves by the opinion of Socrates, of Cato, of Plato, and of St. Clement, but, as you say, they misunderstand the

opinions of these thinkers. And the inhabitants of the
solar city ascribe this to their want of education, since
they are by no means learned in philosophy. Nevertheless, they send abroad to discover the customs of nations,
and the best of these they always adopt. Practice makes
the women suitable for war and other duties. Thus they
agree with Plato, in whom I have read these same things.
The reasoning of our Cajetan does not convince me, and
least of all that of Aristotle. This thing, however, existing among them is excellent and worthy of imitation
— viz, that no physical defect renders a man incapable
of being serviceable except the decrepitude of old age,
since even the deformed are useful for consultation.
The lame serve as guards, watching with the eyes which
they possess. The blind card wool with their hands,
separating the down from the hairs, with which latter
they stuff the couches and sofas; those who are without
the use of eyes and hands give the use of their ears or
their voice for the convenience of the state, and if one
has only one sense, he uses it in the farms. And these
cripples are well treated, and some become spies, telling
the officers of the state what they have heard.

G. M.— Tell me now, I pray you, of their military
affairs. Then you may explain their arts, ways of life
and sciences, and lastly their religion.

Capt.— The triumvir, Power, has under him all the
magistrates of arms, of artillery, of cavalry, of foot
soldiers, of architects, and of strategists, and the masters
and many of the most excellent workmen obey the
magistrates, the men of each art paying allegiance to their
respective chiefs. Moreover, Power is at the head of all
the professors of gymnastics, who teach military exercise,
and who are prudent generals, advanced in age. By
these the boys are trained after their twelfth year.
Before this age, however, they have been accustomed to
wrestling, running, throwing the weight and other minor
exercises, under inferior masters. But at twelve they
are taught how to strike at the enemy, at horses and
elephants, to handle the spear, the sword, the arrow and
the sling; to manage the horse; to advance and to
retreat; to remain in order of battle; to help a comrade

in arms; to anticipate the enemy by cunning; and to conquer.

The women also are taught these arts under their own magistrates and mistresses, so that they may be able if need be to render assistance to the males in battle near the city. They are taught to watch the fortifications lest at some time a hasty attack should suddenly be made. In this respect they praise the Spartans and Amazons. The women know well also how to let fly fiery balls, and how to make them from lead; how to throw stones from pinacles and to go in the way of an attack. They are accustomed also to give up wine unmixed altogether, and that one is punished most severely who shows any fear.

The inhabitants of the City of the Sun do not fear death, because they all believe that the soul is immortal, and that when it has left the body it is associated with other spirits, wicked or good, according to the merits of this present life. Although they are partly followers of Brahma and Pythagoras, they do not believe in the transmigration of souls, except in some cases, by a distinct decree of God. They do not abstain from injuring an enemy of the republic and of religion, who is unworthy of pity. During the second month the army is reviewed, and every day there is practice of arms, either in the cavalry plain or within the walls. Nor are they ever without lectures on the science of war. They take care that the accounts of Moses, of Joshua, of David, of Judas Maccabeus, of Cæsar, of Alexander, of Scipio, of Hannibal, and other great soldiers should be read. And then each one gives his own opinion as to whether these generals acted well or ill, usefully or honorably, and then the teacher answers and says who are right.

G. M.— With whom do they wage war, and for what reasons, since they are so prosperous?

Capt.—Wars might never occur, nevertheless they are exercised in military tactics and in hunting, lest perchance they should become effeminate and unprepared for any emergency. Besides there are four kingdoms in the island, which are very envious of their prosperity, for this reason that the people desire to live after the manner of the inhabitants of the City of the Sun, and to be under their rule rather than that of their own kings. Wherefore the state often makes war upon these because, being neighbors, they are usurpers and live impiously, since they have not an object of worship and do not observe the religion of other nations or of the Brahmins. And other nations of India, to which formerly they were subject, rise up as it were in rebellion, as also do the Taprobanese, whom they wanted to join them at first. The warriors of the City of the Sun, however, are always the victors. As soon as they suffered from insult or disgrace or plunder, or when their allies have been harassed, or a people have been oppressed by a tyrant of the state (for they are always the advocates of liberty), they go immediately to the council for deliberation. After they have knelt in the presence of God that he might inspire their consultation, they procced to examine the merits of the business, and thus war is decided on. Immediately after a priest, whom they call Forensic, is sent away. He demands from the enemy the restitution of the plunder, asks that the allies should be freed from oppression, or that the tyrant should be deposed. If they deny these things war is declared by invoking the vengeance of God — the God of Sabaoth — for destruction of those who maintain an unjust cause. But if the enemy refuse to reply, the priest gives him the space of one hour for his answer, if he is a king, but three if it is a republic, so that they cannot escape giving a response. And in this manner is war undertaken against the insolent enemies of natural rights and of religion. When war has been declared, the deputy of Power performs everything, but Power, like the Roman dictator, plans and wills everything, so that hurtful tardiness may be avoided. And when anything of great moment arises he consults Hoh and Wisdom and Love.

Before this, however, the occasion of war and the justice of making an expedition is declared by a herald in the great council. All from twenty years and upward are admitted to this council, and thus the necessaries are agreed upon. All kinds of weapons stand in the armories, and these they use often in sham fights. The exterior walls of each ring are full of guns prepared by their labors, and they have other engines for hurling which are called cannons, and which they take into battle upon mules and asses and carriages. When they have arrived in an open plain they inclose in the middle the provisions, engines of war, chariots, ladders and machines, and all fight courageously. Then each one returns to the standards, and the enemy thinking that they are giving and preparing to flee, are deceived and relax their order; then the warriors of the City of the Sun, wheeling into wings and columns on each side, regain their breath and strength, and ordering the artillery to discharge their bullets they resume the fight against a disorganized host. And they observe many ruses of this kind. They overcome all mortals with their stratagems and engines. Their camp is fortified after the manner of the Romans. They pitch their tents and fortify with wall and ditch with wonderful quickness. The masters of works, of engines and hurling machines, stand ready, and the soldiers understand the use of the spade and the ax.

Five, eight, or ten leaders learned in the order of battle and in strategy consult together concerning the business of war, and command their bands after consultation. It is their wont to take out with them a body of boys, armed and on horses, so that they may learn to fight, just as the whelps of lions and wolves are accustomed to blood. And these in time of danger betake themselves to a place of safety, along with many armed women. After the battle the women and boys soothe and relieve the pain of the warriors, and wait upon them and encourage them with embraces and pleasant words. How wonderful a help is this! For the soldiers, in order that they may acquit themselves as sturdy men in the eyes of their wives and offspring, endure hardships, and so love makes them conquerors. He who in the fight first scales the enemy's walls receives after the battle a crown of grass, as a token of honor, and at the presentation the women and boys applaud loudly; that one who affords aid to an ally gets a civic crown of oak leaves; he who kills a tyrant dedicates his arms in the temple and receives from

Hoh the cognomen of his deed, and other warriors obtain other kinds of crowns. Every horse soldier carries a spear and two strongly tempered pistols, narrow at the mouth, hanging from his saddle. And to get the barrels of their pistols narrow they pierce the metal which they intend to convert into arms. Further, every cavalry soldier has a sword and a dagger. But the rest, who form the light-armed troops, carry a metal cudgel. For if the foe cannot pierce their metal for pistols and cannot make swords, they attack him with clubs, shatter and overthrow him. Two chains of six spans' length hang from the club, and at the end of these are iron balls, and when these are aimed at the enemy they surround his neck and drag him to the ground; and in order that they may be able to use the club more easily, they do not hold the reins with their hands, but use them by means of the feet. If perchance the reins are interchanged above the trappings of the saddle, the ends are fastened to the stirrups with buckles and not to the feet. And the stirrups have an arrangement for swift movement of the bridle, so that they draw in or let out the rein with marvelous celerity. With the right foot they turn the horse to the left, and with the left to the right. This secret, moreover, is not known to the Tartars. For, although they govern the reins with their feet, they are ignorant nevertheless of turning them and drawing them in and letting them out by means of the block of the stirrups. The light-armed cavalry with them are the first to engage in battle, then the men forming the phalanx with their spears, then the archers for whose services a great price is paid, and who are accustomed to fight in lines crossing one another as the threads of cloth, some rushing forward in their turn and others receding. They have a band of lancers strengthening the line of battle, but they make trial of the swords only at the end.

After the battle they celebrate the military triumphs after the manner of the Romans, and even in a more magnificent way. Prayers by the way of thank-offerings are made to God, and then the general presents himself in the temple, and the deeds, good and bad, are related by the poet or historian, who according to custom was with the expedition. And the greatest chief, Hoh, crowns the general with laurel and distributes little gifts and honors to all the valorous soldiers, who are for some days free from public duties. But this exemption from work is by no means pleasing to them, since they know not what it is to be at leisure, and so they help their companions. On the other hand, they who have been conquered through their own fault, or have lost the victory, are blamed; and they who were the first to take to flight are in no way worthy to escape death, unless when the whole army asks their lives, and each one takes upon himself a part of their punishment. But this indulgence is rarely granted, except when there are good reasons favoring it. But he who did not bear help to an ally or friend is beaten with rods. That one who did not obey orders is given to the beasts, in an inclosure, to be devoured, and a staff is put in his hand, and if he should conquer the lions and the bears that are there, which is almost impossible, he is received into favor again. The conquered states or those willingly delivered up to them, forthwith have all things in common, and receive a garrison and magistrates from the City of the Sun, and by degrees they are accustomed to the ways of the city, the mistress of all, to which they even send their sons to be taught without contributing anything for expense.

It would be too great trouble to tell you about the spies and their master, and about the guards and laws and ceremonies, both within and without the state, which you can of yourself imagine. Since from childhood they are chosen according to their inclination and the star under which they were born, therefore each one working according to his natural propensity, does his duty well and pleasantly, because naturally. The same things I may say concerning strategy and the other functions. There are guards in the city by day and by night, and they are placed at the four gates, and outside the walls of the seventh ring, above the breastworks and towers and inside mounds. These places are guarded in the day by women, in the night by men. And lest the guard should become weary of watching, and in case of a surprise, they change them every three hours, as is the custom with our soldiers. At sunset, when the drum and symphonia sound, the armed guards are distributed. Cavalry and infantry make use of hunting as the symbol of war, and practice games and hold festivities in the plains. Then the music strikes up, and freely they pardon the offenses and faults of the enemy, and after the victories they are kind to them, if it has been decreed that they should destroy the walls of the enemy's city and take their lives. All these things are done in the same day as the victory, and afterward they never cease to load the conquered with favors, for they say that there ought to be no fighting, except when the conquerors give up the conquered, not when they kill them. If there is a dispute among them concerning injury or any other matter (for they themselves scarcely ever contend except in matters of honor), the chief and his magistrates chastise the accused one secretly, if he has done harm in deeds after he has been first angry. If they wait until the time of the battle for the verbal decision, they must give vent to their anger against the enemy, and he who in battle shows the most daring deeds is considered to have defended the better and truer cause in the struggle, and the other yields, and they are punished justly. Nevertheless, they are not allowed to come to single combat, since right is maintained by the tribunal, and because the unjust cause is often apparent when the more just succumbs, and he who professes to be the better man shows this in public fight.

G. M.—This is worth while, so that factions should not be cherished for the harm of the fatherland, and so that civil wars might not occur, for by means of these a tyrant often arises, as the examples of Rome and Athens show. Now, I pray you, tell me of their works and matter connected therewith.

Capt.—I believe that you have already heard about their military affairs and about their agricultural and pastoral life, and in what way these are common to them, and how they honor with the first grade of nobility whoever is considered to have a knowledge of these. They who are skillful in more arts than these they consider still nobler, and they set that one apart for teaching the art in which he is most skillful. The occupations which require the most labor, such as working in metals and building, are the most praiseworthy among them. No one declines to go to these occupations, for the reason that from the beginning their propensities are well known, and among them, on account of the distribution of labor, no one does work harmful to him, but only that which is necessary for him. The occupations entailing less labor belong to the women. All of them are expected to know how to swim, and for this reason ponds are dug outside the walls of the city and within them near to the fountains.

Commerce is of little use to them, but they know the value of money and they count for the use of their ambassadors and explorers, so that with it they may have the means of living. They receive merchants into their states from the different countries of the world, and these buy the superfluous goods of the city. The people of the City of the Sun refuse to take money, but in importing they accept in exchange those things of which they are in need, and sometimes they buy with money; and the young people in the City of the Sun are much amused when they see that for a small price they receive so many things in exchange. The old men however, do not laugh. They are unwilling that the state should be corrupted by the vicious customs of slaves and foreigners. Therefore they do business at the gates, and sell those whom they have taken in war or keep them for digging ditches and other hard work without the city, and for this reason they always send four bands of soldiers to take care of the fields, and with them there are the laborers. They go out of the four gates from which roads with walls on both sides of them lead to the sea, so that goods might easily be carried over them and foreigners might not meet with difficulty on their way.

To strangers they are kind and polite; they keep them for three days at the public expense; after they have first washed their feet, they show them their city and its customs, and they honor them with a seat at the council and public table, and there are men whose duty it is to take care of and guard the guests. But if strangers should wish to become citizens of their state, they try them first for a month on a farm, and for another month in the city, then they decide concerning them, and admit them with certain ceremonies and oaths.

Agriculture is much followed among them; there is not a span of earth without cultivation, and they observe the winds and propitious stars. With the exception of a few left in the city all go out armed, and with flags and drums and trumpets sounding, to the fields, for the purpose of plowing, sowing, digging, hoeing, reaping, gathering fruit and grapes; and they set in order everything, and do their work in a very few hours and with much care. They use wagons fitted with sails which are borne along by the wind even when it is contrary, by the marvelous contrivance of wheels within wheels.

And when there is no wind a beast draws along a huge cart, which is a grand sight.

The guardians of the land move about in the meantime, armed and always in their proper turn. They do not use dung and filth for manuring the fields, thinking that the fruit contracts something of their rottenness, and when eaten gives a short and poor subsistence, as women who are beautiful with rouge and from want of exercise bring forth feeble offspring. Wherefore they do not as it were paint the earth, but dig it up well and use secret remedies, so that fruit is borne quickly and multiplies, and is not destroyed. They have a book for this work, which they call the Georgics. As much of the land as is necessary is cultivated, and the rest is used for the pasturage of cattle.

The excellent occupation of breeding and rearing horses, oxen, sheep, dogs, and all kinds of domestic and tame animals, is in the highest esteem among them as it was in the time of Abraham. And the animals are led so to pair that they may be able to breed well.

Fine pictures of oxen, horses, sheep, and other animals are placed before them. They do not turn out horses with mares to feed, but at the proper time they bring them together in an inclosure of the stables in their fields. And this is done when they observe that the constellation Archer is in favorable conjunction with Mars and Jupiter. For the oxen they observe the Bull, for the sheep the Ram, and so on in accordance with art. Under the Pleiades they keep a drove of hens and ducks and geese, which are driven out by the women to feed near the city. The women only do this when it is a pleasure to them. There are also places inclosed, where they make cheese, butter, and milk food. They also keep capons, fruit, and other things, and for all these matters there is a book which they call the Bucolics. They have an abundance of all things, since every one likes to be industrious, their labors being slight and profitable. They are docile, and that one among them who is head of the rest in duties of this kind they call king. For they say that this is the proper name of the leaders, and it does not belong to ignorant persons. It is wonderful to see how men and women march together collectively, and always in obedience to the voice of the king. Nor do they regard him with loathing as we do, for they know that although he is greater than themselves, he is for all that their father and brother. They keep groves and woods for wild animals, and they often hunt.

The science of navigation is considered very dignified by them, and they possess rafts and triremes, which go over the waters without rowers or the force of the wind, but by a marvelous contrivance. And other vessels they have which are moved by the winds. They have a correct knowledge of the stars, and of the ebb and flow of the tide. They navigate for the sake of becoming acquainted with nations and different countries and things. They injure nobody, and they do not put up with injury, and they never go to battle unless when provoked. They assert that the whole earth will in time come to live in accordance with their customs, and consequently they always find out whether there be a nation whose manner of living is better and more approved than the rest. They admire the Christian institutions and look for a realization of the apostolic life in vogue among themselves and in us. There are treaties between them and the Chinese, and many other nations, both insular and continental, such as Siam and Calicut, which they are only just able to explore. Furthermore, they have artificial fires, bat-

tles on sea and land, and many strategic secrets. Therefore they are nearly always victorious.

G. M.—Now it would be very pleasant to learn with
what foods and drinks they are nourished, and in what
way and for how long they live.

Capt.—Their food consists of flesh, butter, honey, cheese,
garden herbs, and vegetables of various kinds. They
were unwilling at first to slay animals, because it seemed
cruel; but thinking afterward that it was also cruel to destroy herbs which have a share of sensitive feeling, they
saw that they would perish from hunger unless they did
an unjustifiable action for the sake of justifiable ones,
and so now they all eat meat. Nevertheless, they do not
kill willingly useful animals, such as oxen and horses.
They observe the difference between useful and harmful
foods, and for this they employ the science of medicine.
They always change their food. First they eat flesh, then
fish, then afterward they go back to flesh, and nature is
never incommoded or weakened. The old people use the
more digestible kind of food, and take three meals a day,
eating only a little. But the general community eat twice,
and the boys four times, that they might satisfy nature.
The length of their lives is generally one hundred years,
but often they reach two hundred.

As regards drinking, they are extremely moderate.
Wine is never given to young people until they are ten
years old, unless the state of their health demands it.
After their tenth year they take it diluted with water,
and so do the women, but the old men of fifty and upward use little or no water. They eat the most healthy
things, according to the time of the year.

They think nothing harmful which is brought forth by
God, except when there has been abuse by taking too
much. And therefore in the summer they feed on fruits,
because they are moist and juicy and cool, and counteract the heat and dryness. In the winter they feed on dry
articles, and in the autumn they eat grapes, since they
are given by God to remove melancholy and sadness; and
they also make use of scents to a great degree. In the
morning, when they have all risen, they comb their hair
and wash their faces and hands with cold water. Then

they chew thyme or rock parsley or fennel, or rub their hands with these plants. The old men make incense, and with their faces to the east repeat the short prayer which Jesus Christ taught us. After this they go to wait upon the old men, some go to the dance, and others to the duties of the state. Later on they meet at the early lectures, then in the temple, then for bodily exercise. Then for a little while they sit down to rest, and at length they go to dinner.

Among them there is never gout in the hands or feet, no catarrh, no sciatica, nor grievous colics, nor flatulency, nor hard breathing. For these diseases are caused by indigestion and flatulency, and by frugality and exercise they remove every humor and spasm. Wherefore it is unseemly in the extreme to be seen vomiting or spitting, since they say that this is a sign either of little exercise or of ignoble sloth, or of drunkenness or gluttony. They suffer rather from swellings or from the dry spasm, which they relieve with plenty of good and juicy food. They heal fevers with pleasant baths and with milk food, and with a pleasant habitation in the country and by gradual exercise. Unclean diseases cannot be prevalent with them because they often clean their bodies by bathing in wine, and soothe them with aromatic oil, and by the sweat of exercise they diffuse the poisonous vapor which corrupts the blood and the marrow. They do suffer a little from consumption, because they cannot perspire at the breast, but they never have asthma, for the humid nature of which a heavy man is required. They cure hot fevers with cold potations of water, but slight ones with sweet smells, with cheese bread or sleep, with music or dancing. Tertiary fevers are cured by bleeding, by rhubarb or by a similar drawing remedy, or by water soaked in the roots of plants, with purgative and sharp-tasting qualities. But it is rarely that they take purgative medicines. Fevers occurring every fourth day are cured easily by suddenly startling the unprepared patients, and by means of herbs producing effects opposite to the humors of this fever. All these secrets they told me in opposition to their own wishes. They take more diligent pains to cure the lasting fevers, which they fear more, and they strive to counteract these by the observation of stars and of plants, and by prayers to God. Fevers recurring every fifth, sixth, eighth or more days, you never find whenever heavy humors are wanting.

They use baths, and moreover they have warm ones according to the Roman custom, and they make use also of olive oil. They have found out, too, a great many secret cures for the preservation of cleanliness and health. And in other ways they labor to cure the epilepsy, with which they are often troubled.

G. M. — A sign this disease is of wonderful cleverness, for from it Hercules, Scotus, Socrates, Callimachus and Mahomet have suffered.

Capt. — They cure by means of prayers to heaven, by strengthening the head, by acids, by planned gymnastics, and with fat cheese bread sprinkled with the flour of wheaten corn. They are very skilled in making dishes, and in them they put spice, honey, butter and many highly strengthening spices, and they temper their richness with acids, so that they never vomit. They do not drink ice-cold drinks nor artificial hot drinks, as the Chinese do; for they are not without aid against the humors of the body, on account of the help they get from the natural heat of the water; but they strengthen it with crushed garlic, with vinegar, with wild thyme, with mint, and with basil, in the summer or in time of special heaviness. They know also a secret for renovating life after about the seventieth year, and for ridding it of affliction, and this they do by a pleasing and indeed wonderful art.

G. M. — Thus far you have said nothing concerning their sciences and magistrates.

Capt. — Undoubtedly I have. But since you are so curious I will add more. Both when it is new moon and full moon they call a council after a sacrifice. To this all from twenty years upward are admitted, and each one is asked separately to say what is wanting in the state, and which of the magistrates have discharged their duties rightly and which wrongly. Then after eight days all the magistrates assemble, to wit, Hoh first, and with him Power, Wisdom and Love. Each one of the three last has three magistrates under him, making in all thirteen, and they consider the affairs of the arts pertaining to each one of them; Power, of war; Wisdom, of the sciences; Love, of food, clothing, education and breeding. The masters of all the bands, who are captains of tens, of fifties, of hundreds, also assemble, the women first and then the men. They argue about those things which are for the welfare of the state, and they choose the magistrates from among those who have already been named in the great council. In this manner they assemble daily, Hoh and his three princes, and they correct, confirm and execute the matters passing to them, as decisions in the elections; other necessary questions they provide of themselves. They do not use lots unless when they are altogether doubtful how to decide. The eight magistrates under Hoh, Power, Wisdom and Love are changed according to the wish of the people, but the first four are never changed, unless they, taking council with themselves, give up the dignity of one to another, whom among them they know to be wiser, more renowned, and more nearly perfect. And then they are obedient and honorable, since they yield willingly to the wiser man and are taught by him. This, however, rarely happens. The principals of the sciences, except Metaphysics, who is Hoh himself, and is as it were the architect of all science, having rule over all, are attached to Wisdom. Hoh is ashamed to be ignorant of any possible thing. Under Wisdom therefore is Grammar, Logic, Physics, Medicine, Astrology, Astronomy, Geometry, Cosmography, Music, Perspective, Arithmetic, Poetry, Rhetoric, Painting, Sculpture. Under the triumvir Love are Breeding, Agriculture, Education, Medicine, Clothing, Pasturage, Coining.

G. M.— What about their judges?

Capt.— This is the point I was just thinking of explaining. Everyone is judged by the first master of his trade, and thus all the head artificers are judges. They punish with exile, with flogging, with blame, with deprivation of the common table, with exclusion from the church and from the company of women. When there is a case in which great injury has been done, it is punished with death, and they repay an eye with an eye, a nose for a nose, a tooth for a tooth, and so on, according to the law of retaliation. If the offense is willful the council decides. When there is strife and it takes place unde-signedly, the sentence is mitigated; nevertheless, not by the judge but by the triumvirate, from whom even it may be referred to Hoh, not on account of justice but of mercy, for Hoh is able to pardon. They have no prisons, except one tower for shutting up rebellious enemies, and there is no written statement of a case, which we com-monly call a lawsuit. But the accusation and witnesses are produced in the presence of the judge and Power; the accused person makes his defense, and he is immediately acquitted or condemned by the judge; and if he appeals to the triumvirate, on the following day he is acquitted or condemned. On the third day he is dismissed through the mercy and clemency of Hoh, or receives the inviola-ble rigor of his sentence. An accused person is recon-ciled to his accuser and to his witnesses, as it were, with the medicine of his complaint, that is, with embracing and kissing. No one is killed or stoned unless by the hands of the people, the accuser and the witnesses beginning first. For they have no executioners and lictors, lest the state should sink into ruin. The choice of death is given to the rest of the people, who inclose the lifeless remains in little bags and burn them by the application of fire, while exhorters are present for the pur-pose of advising concerning a good death. Nevertheless, the whole nation laments and beseeches God that his anger may be appeased, being in grief that it should, as it were, have to cut off a rotten member of the state. Certain officers talk to and convince the accused man by means of arguments until he himself acquiesces in the sentence of death passed upon him, or else he does not die. But if a crime has been committed against the liberty of the republic, or against God, or against the supreme magistrates, there is immediate censure without pity. These only are punished with death. He who is about to die is compelled to state in the presence of the people and with religious scrupulousness the reasons for which he does not deserve death, and also the sins of the others who ought to die instead of him, and further the mistakes of the magistrates. If, moreover, it should seem right to the person thus asserting, he must say why the accused ones are deserving of less punishment than he. And if by his arguments he gains the victory he is sent into exile, and appeases the state by means of prayers and sacrifices and good life ensuing. They do not torture those named by the accused person, but they warn them. Sins of frailty and ignorance are punished only with blaming, and with compulsory continuation as learners under the law and discipline of those sciences or arts against which they have sinned. And all these things they have mutually among themselves, since they seem to be in very truth members of the same body, and one of another.

This further I would have you know, that if a transgressor, without waiting to be accused, goes of his own accord before a magistrate, accusing himself and seeking to make amends, that one is liberated from the punishment of a secret crime, and since he has not been accused of such a crime, his punishment is changed into another. They take special care that no one should invent slander, and if this should happen they meet the offense with the punishment of retaliation. Since they always walk about and work in crowds, five witnesses are required for the conviction of a transgressor. If the case is otherwise, after having theatened him, he is released after he has sworn an oath as the warrant of good conduct. Or if he is accused a second or third time, his increased punishment rests on the testimony of three or two witnesses. They have but few laws, and these short and plain, and written upon a flat table, and hanging to the doors of the temple, that is between the columns. And on single columns can be seen the essence of things described in the very terse style of Metaphysics — viz, the essences of God, of the angels, of the world, of the stars, of man, of fate, of virtue, all done with great wisdom. The definitions of all the virtues are also delineated here, and here is the tribunal, where the judges of all the virtues have their seat. The definition of a certain virtue is writtten under that column where the judges for the aforesaid virtue sit.

and when a judge gives judgment he sits and speaks thus: O
son, thou hast sinned against this sacred definition of benefi-
cence, or of magnanimity, or of another virtue, as the
case may be. And after discussion the judge legally con-
demns him to the punishment for the crime of which he
is accused — viz, for injury, for despondency, for pride,
for ingratitude, for sloth, etc. But the sentences are
certain and true correctives, savoring more of clemency
than of actual punishment.

G. M. — Now you ought to tell me about their priests,
their sacrifices, their religion, and their belief.

Capt. — The chief priest is Hoh, and it is the duty of
all the superior magistrates to pardon sins. Therefore
the whole state by secret confession, which we also use,
tell their sins to the magistrates, who at once purge their
souls and teach those that are inimical to the people.
Then the sacred magistrates themselves confess their
own sinfulness to the three supreme chiefs, and together
they confess the faults of one another, though no special
one is named, and they confess especially the heavier
faults and those harmful to the state. At length the
triumvirs confess their sinfulness to Hoh himself, who
forthwith recognizes the kinds of sins that are harmful
to the state, and succors with timely remedies. Then he
offers sacrifices and prayers to God. And before this he
confesses the sins of the whole people, in the presence
of God, and publicly in the temple, above the altar, as
often as it had been necessary that the fault should be
corrected. Nevertheless, no transgressor is spoken of by
his name. In this manner he absolves the people by
advising them that they should beware of sins of the
aforesaid kind. Afterward he offers sacrifice to God,
that he should pardon the state and absolve it of its
sins, and to teach and defend it. Once in every year
the chief priests of each separate subordinate state confess their sins in the presence of Hoh. Thus he is not
ignorant of the wrongdoings of the provinces, and forthwith he removes them with all human and heavenly
remedies.

Sacrifice is conducted after the following manner: Hoh
asks the people which one among them wishes to give

himself as a sacrifice to God for the sake of his fellows. He is then placed upon the fourth table, with ceremonies and the offering up of prayers: the table is hung up in a wonderful manner by means of four ropes passing through four cords attached to firm pulley blocks in the small dome of the temple. This done they cry to the God of mercy, that he may accept the offering, not of a beast as among the heathen, but of a human being. Then Hoh orders the ropes to be drawn and the sacrifice is pulled up above to the centre of the small dome, and there it dedicates itself with the most fervent supplications. Food is given to it through a window by the priests, who live around the dome, but it is allowed a very little to eat, until it has atoned for the sins of the state. There with prayer and fasting he cries to the God of heaven that he might accept its willing offering. And after twenty or thirty days, the anger of God being appeased, the sacrifice becomes a priest, or sometimes, though rarely, returns below by means of the outer way for the priests. Ever after this man is treated with great benevolence and much honor, for the reason that he offered himself unto death for the sake of his country. But God does not require death. The priests above twenty-four years of age offer praises from their places in the top of the temple. This they do in the middle of the night, at noon, in the morning and in the evening, to wit, four times a day they sing their chants in the presence of God. It is also their work to observe the stars and to note with the astrolabe their motions and influences upon human things, and to find out their powers. Thus they know in what part of the earth any change has been or will be, and at what time it has taken place, and they send to find whether the matter be as they have it. They make a note of predictions, true and false, so that they may be able from experience to predict most correctly. The priests, moreover, determine the hours for breeding and the days for sowing, reaping, and gathering the vintage, and are as it were the ambassadors and intercessors and connection between God and man. And it is from among them mostly that Hoh is elected. They write very learned treatises and search into the sciences. Below they never descend, unless for their dinner and supper, so that the essence of their heads do not descend to the stomachs and liver. Only very seldom, and that as a cure for the ills of solitude, do they have converse with women. On certain days Hoh goes up to them and deliberates with them concerning the matters which he has lately investigated for the benefit of the state and all the nations of the world.

In the temple beneath one priest always stands near the altar praying for the people, and at the end of every hour another succeeds him, just as we are accustomed in solemn prayer to change every fourth hour. And this method of supplication they call perpetual prayer. After a meal they return thanks to God. Then they sing the deeds of the Christian, Jewish, and Gentile heroes, and of those of all other nations, and this is very delightful to them. Forsooth, no one is envious of another. They sing a hymn to Love, one to Wisdom, and one each to all the other virtues, and this they do under the direction of the ruler of each virtue. Each one takes the woman he loves most, and they dance for exercise with propriety and stateliness under the peristyles. The women wear their long hair all twisted together and collected into one knot on the crown of the head, but in rolling it they leave one curl. The men, however, have one curl only and the rest of their hair around the head is shaven off. Further, they wear a slight covering, and above this a round hat a little larger than the size of their head. In the fields they use caps, but at home each one wears a biretto white, red, or another color according to his trade or occupation. Moreover, the magistrates use grander and more imposing-looking coverings for the head.

They hold great festivities when the sun enters the four cardinal points of the heavens, that is, when he enters Cancer, Libra, Capricorn, and Aries. On these occasions they have very learned, splendid, and as it were comic performances. They celebrate also every full and every new moon with a festival, as also they do the anniversaries of the founding of the city, and of the days when they have won victories or done any other great

achievement. The celebrations take place with the music
of female voices, with the noise of trumpets and drums,
and the firing of salutations. The poets sing the praises
of the most renowned leaders and the victories. Nevertheless if any of them should deceive even by dispar-
aging a foreign hero, he is punished. No one can
exercise the function of a poet who invents that which is not
true, and a license like this they think to be a pest of
our world, for the reason that it puts a premium upon
virtue and often assigns it to unworthy persons, either
from fear or flattery, or ambition or avarice. For the
praise of no one is a statue erected until after his death;
but while he is alive, who has found out new arts and
very useful secrets, or who has rendered great service to
the state, either at home or on the battlefield, his name
is written in the book of heroes. They do not bury
dead bodies, but burn them, so that a plague may not
arise from them, and so that they may be converted into
fire, a very noble and powerful thing which has its coming from the sun and returns to it. And for the above
reasons no chance is given for idolatry. The statues and
pictures of the heroes, however, are there, and the
splendid women set apart to become mothers often look
at them. Prayers are made from the state to the four
horizontal corners of the world. In the morning to the
rising sun, then to the setting sun, then to the south
and lastly to the north; and in the contrary order in the
evening, first to the setting sun, to the rising sun, to
the north, and at length to the south. They repeat but
one prayer, which asks for health of body and of mind
and happiness for themselves and all people, and they
conclude it with the petition " As it seems best to God."
The public prayer for all is long, and it is poured forth
to heaven. For this reason the altar is round and is divided crosswise by ways at right angles to one another.
By these ways Hoh enters after he has repeated the four
prayers, and he prays looking up to heaven. And then
a great mystery is seen by them. The priestly vest-
ments are of a beauty and meaning like to those of
Aaron. They resemble Nature and they surpass Art.
They divide the seasons according to the revolution of

the sun, and not of the stars, and they observe yearly by how much time the one precedes the other. They hold that the sun approaches nearer and nearer, and therefore by ever-lessening circles reaches the tropics and the equator every year a little sooner. They measure months by the course of the moon, years by that of the sun. They praise Ptolemy, admire Copernicus, but place Aristarchus and Philolaus before him. They take great pains in endeavoring to understand the construction of the world, and whether or not it will perish, and at what time. They believe that the true oracle of Jesus Christ is by the signs in the sun, in the moon, and in the stars, which signs do not thus appear to many of us foolish ones. Therefore they wait for the renewing of the age, and perchance for its end. They say that it is very doubtful whether the world was made from nothing, or from the ruins of other worlds, or from chaos, but they certainly think that it was made, and did not exist from eternity. Therefore they disbelieve in Aristotle, whom they consider a logician and not a philosopher. From analogies, they can draw many arguments against the eternity of the world. The sun and the stars they, so to speak, regard as the living representatives and signs of God, as the temples and holy living altars, and they honor but do not worship them. Beyond all other things they venerate the sun, but they consider no created thing worthy the adoration of worship. This they give to God alone, and thus they serve him, that they may not come into the power of a tyrant and fall into misery by undergoing punishment by creatures of revenge. They contemplate and know God under the image of the Sun and they call it the sign of God, his face and living image, by means of which light, heat, life, and the making of all things good and bad proceeds. Therefore they have built an altar like to the Sun in shape, and the priests praise God in the Sun and in the stars, as it were his altars, and in the heavens, his temple as it were; and they pray to good angels, who are, so to speak, the intercessors living in the stars, their strong abodes. For God long since set signs of their beauty in heaven, and of his glory in the Sun. They say there is but one heaven, and that the planets move and rise of themselves when they approach the sun, or are in conjunction with it.

They assert two principles of the physics of things below, namely, that the Sun is the father, and the Earth the mother; the air is an impure part of the heavens; all fire is derived from the sun. The sea is the sweat of earth, or the fluid of earth combusted, and fused within its bowels; but is the bond of union between air and earth, as the blood is of the spirit and flesh of animals. The world is a great animal, and we live within it as worms live within us. Therefore we do not belong to the system of stars, sun, and earth, but to God only; for in respect to them which seek only to amplify themselves, we are born and live by chance; but in respect to God, .whose instruments we are, we are formed by prescience and design, and for a high end. Therefore we are bound to no Father but God, and receive all things from him. They hold as beyond question the immortality of souls, and that these associate with good angels after death, or with bad angels, according as they have likened themselves in this life to either. For all things seek their like. They differ little from us as to places of reward and punishment. They are in doubt whether there are other worlds beyond ours, and account it madness to say there is nothing. Nonentity is incompatible with the infinite entity of God. They lay down two principles of metaphysics, entity which is the highest God, and nothingness which is the defect of entity. Evil and sin come of the propensity to nothingness; the sin having its cause not efficient, but in deficiency. Deficiency is, they say, of power, wisdom or will. Sin they place in the last of these three, because he who knows and has the power to do good is bound also to have the will, for will arises out of them. They worship God in Trinity, saying God is the supreme Power, whence proceeds the highest Wisdom, which is the same with God, and from these comes Love, which is both Power and Wisdom; but they do not distinguish persons by name, as in our Christian law, which has not been revealed to them. This religion, when its abuses have been removed, will be the future mistress of the world, as great theologians teach and hope. Therefore Spain found the New World (though its first discoverer, Columbus, greatest of heroes, was a Genoese), that all nations should be gathered under one law. We know not what we do, but God knows, whose instruments we are. They sought new regions for lust of gold and riches, but God works to a higher end. The sun strives to burn up the earth, not to produce plants and men, but God guides the battle to great issues. His the praise, to him the glory!

G. M.— Oh, if you knew what our astrologers say of the coming age, and of our age, that has in it more history within a hundred years than all the world had in four thousand years before! Of the wonderful invention of printing and guns, and the use of the magnet, and how it all comes of Mercury, Mars, the Moon, and the Scorpion!

Capt.— Ah, well! God gives all in his good time. They astrologize too much.